SIMPLE MATH ~~ FOR AD

Learning Essential Math Skills:
Add, Subtract, Multiply, Divide, Time, Calendar, Count Money, Percent, Average, Estimate, Ratios, Economics, Inflation, Mortgage, Loan Finance, Amortize, Practice Problems and More - Absorb

by

Ralph Koerber

COPYRIGHT

~~~~~~~~~~~~~~~~~~~

DISCLOSURE

The content in this text predates the teaching and learning theories of Common Core Math and in no way presumes to negate it or its focus or in any way be in conflict with Common Core Math.

The Common Core State Standards (CCSS) are a set of academic standards in mathematics and English language arts/literacy (ELA) developed under the direction of the Council of Chief State School Officers (CCSSO) and the National Governors Association (NGA).

You are encouraged to comply with these standards in all respects. It is believed the standards are an expansion and clarification of this text with new methods being taught in some elementary classes.

We adults learned *simple math* and still use math in a manner different from today's teachings and that is OK. This book provides a brush-up and a how-to do *simple math*.

ACKNOWLEDGEMENT

Thank you to my Mother and Father
for giving me the gift of education,
a thirst for knowledge and experience,
and their undying encouragement and guidance,
all of which prepared me to consistently become a better person,
sharing to the benefit of others.

Endless thanks to my beautiful lady. My wife is the jewel in my crown.
She supports my passion to share my knowledge and experience.
She is my Editor, again. This is the twelfth book.
She is my Rock.

My thanks also flow to Scott Allan, my Coach,
for his guidance during my early months with
Self-Publishing School,
where I learned the hows and whys of self-publishing.

BOOKS BY YOUR AUTHOR

SERIES: *DREAMS FULFILLED*

1. Road to Journey's End

2. Sail of a Lifetime

3. Inspirational Invocations and Addresses

4. Mother's Recipes

5. Semester at Sea – Global Voyage of Discovery

6. Teen Handbook and Workbook - For Your New Life

7. College Student Handbook and Workbook – Guidance and Discussion

8. Adult and Parent Handbook – Guidance and Discussion supporting Middle School Families and Students

9. Adult Handbook and Workbook – A Discussion on Self-Improvement and Relationships

10. Change Your Mindset and Enhance Your Future

11. Simple Math Workbook – Learning Essential Math Skills

12. This New Release November 2022

Your Author's Bookshelf at the back of this book
provides a glimpse into each of these books.
You are encouraged to see for yourself which book
may call to you.
The books are available on Amazon.com

SIMPLE MATH WORKBOOK FOR ADULTS

Learning Essential Math Skills:
Add, Subtract, Multiply, Divide, Time, Calendar, Count Money, Percent, Average, Estimate, Ratios, Economics, Inflation, Mortgage, Loan Finance, Amortize, Practice Problems and More - Absorb

CONTENTS

Copyright

Disclosure

Acknowledgement

Series: Dreams Fulfilled – eleven books

Contents

Dedication

Opening Remarks

Introduction

Poem – Read Down, then Up

Class is in Session

Contract

Exercise One

    - Whole Numbers
    - Count Up to 120 from 1 by X
    - Count Down from 120 to 1 by X
    - Count and Recount – Exercises 1-A through 1-X

    Count Money and Read Numbers

    Sidelight Lesson – Fuel Price

Exercise Two

- 2-A Addition
- 2-B Subtraction
- Addition – Subtraction Relationship
- Proving Calculation

Exercise Three

- 3-A Multiplication
- Shortcuts
- 3-B Times Tables
- Times Table Chart
- 3-C Division
- Multiplication – Division Relationship

Exercise Four

- 4-A Fractions – Proper
- 4-B Fractions - Improper
- 4-C Decimal Equivalents
- 4-D Decimal Equivalents Chart
- 4-E Averages
- 4-F Estimating
- 4-G Rounding
- 4-H Ratios
- 4-I Reciprocal
- 4-J Percentages
- 4-K Measure
- 4-L Time Management
- 4-M Calendar
- 4-N Weather Map Interpretation

Exercise Five

- Common Calculation Challenges

SIMPLE MATH WORKBOOK
FOR ADULTS

DEDICATION

This book is Dedicated to Emma. She lives in Florida.
Emma is a student close to my heart. She is committed to learning
Simple Math. She will continue to do her best as she matures to
adulthood. Do your best to learn with her, as she is on her way.

~~~~

This book is also dedicated to you. It is in your hands because you may
be curious and/or willing to explore and expand your friendship with
simple math. It is dedicated to your sisters and brothers, also willing to
explore themselves and their attitudes toward math. This book may
serve as a refresher for many adults. It offers a challenge to you. It is
up to you to accept the challenge as a self-improvement challenge.
When you adopt a self-improvement challenge and achieve, you grow
exponentially.

Your inner self is waiting to work on understanding math and may be
patiently waiting for change. The fast pace of our world drowns out the
loud cry of the inner self for attention and nourishment. Hear the
desperate call.

Your invitation of math into your mind as a welcome presence will
both stimulate and support your thinking processes and may serve
you well. Learn, visualize, and understand math without memorizing.

OPENING REMARKS

Hello adults,

You are about to begin an adventure of review intended to give you a brush-up of the principles of *simple math*. You are to be commended for getting this book and being ready to cover *simple math* material. Each of us is a student. You are a student in review of math. So, put on your thinking cap.

What we will do is review and strengthen your level of math through a series of simple exercises designed to give you something to build upon as we progressively move from one focus point to another, while you absorb the information and exercises at your own pace. Slow and steady, coupled with your commitment to learn, will win for you your sense of understanding of *simple math* and give you a comfort level as you progress, understand, and become more familiar with the material.

This book offers you a self-challenge. Accept your self-challenge for yourself and your self-improvement. We grow as individuals when we accept self-challenges and achieve. You will sense your personal growth and increased comfort as you move through the exercises in this book.

INTRODUCTION

Each of us is a student. You are able to learn this *simple math*.
These are the fundamentals on which higher math is built.
Master these basic principles and techniques. Think without distraction.
See through the exercises and what they show you.
Visualize a problem. Repeat the calculations. After you repeat the
exercises and understand the concepts and formulas, you may see the
answer in your mind before you arrive at it on paper. Clarity comes with
focus and practice.

Schedule certain hours during daytime as your study time to allow
yourself sufficient time to focus on absorbing this material. Your
conscious intention and self-discipline in doing this will support your
learning and unlock your potential to know and master simple math.
Select your quiet space for study; have pencil and paper ready and give
yourself an uninterrupted study hour before taking a refreshing break.
Transfer the exercise problems to your own paper and begin. You may
come to know that writing out the problem on your paper makes it more-
real and understandable for you.

We seek to improve. Practice with these exercises leads to
improvement in thought, understanding and attitude toward *simple
math*. When you practice and continue to apply what you learn
sequentially in this book, you will better understand and relate to how
numbers are in your daily life.

You can make friends with math. You are able to understand math.
You need to decide these two positions apply to you. Only you decide.
Other people offer the position of positive support for you.

You are accountable to yourself. When you become accountable and
move yourself to become a master of *simple math,* your ability to solve
math and other problems multiplies exponentially.

The exercises in this book are planned sequential steps forward as guides for you. They will share the concepts, formulas and shortcuts for you to think about, learn and absorb, work through and understand. Some exercise problems may contain more numbers or information than you need to solve the problem. Visualize the problem as presented and you will see the lead toward the solution.

Work each problem thoughtfully so that you understand.
Put away your electronics and calculators. Think for yourself.
Rely on yourself and your ability to learn and master *simple math*.
This way you learn and do by thinking through the lessons that apply to each type of problem. Remember, these are problems we face every day. So, you are better-preparing yourself for each day by learning, through your dedication, to totally understanding each problem. The problems in this book build on the previous. So, be sure you understand and are able to recall the principles and processes shared. These are simple formulas for handling and solving daily problems.

Ask for help to understand, when you feel the appropriateness and need. Generally, it is a mistake to not ask for help for understanding. Clarity of thought is rooted in many discussions and explanations. Be sure you ask. The wrong question is the one not asked.

Set aside each and every distraction so you can focus as though you were in a classroom with me. Focus your thoughts. You create your classroom by shutting out distractions, so you can focus and think only about the problem to be understood and solved. When you do this, you gift yourself with an outcome that will be long-lasting and give you an immeasurable advantage as you improve your math competence.

Rest assured that I do know about learning and the importance of self-review. I faced a grueling challenge preparing for the CPA Exam. It is unlike other exams. It is a 5-part, 3-day, 21-hour exam. I prepared myself well and reviewed and succeeded. My encouragement to you is to persevere, think, see the logic in the numbers in math, work each problem, repeat working the problems, and master *simple math* because you are here to do it and the time is now. You can do this. You can learn math.

I can share, show you, explain, give examples and exercises and trust you to help govern yourself. You have to govern your thinking through each problem by your manually working through the thoughtful steps to the solution.

That is why you are reading and committing to working in this book - to do what it takes. You can do this. When you decide you can do this, you are right and on track. If you were to decide you could not do this, you are also right. Be sure you make the best long-term positive decision for yourself so you stay on track.

I can write and encourage you. The hard work is for you to do.
Your reward comes at the end. Your reward will be proportional to your commitment to the process of learning. So, the outcome is up to you alone. You will gain as a result of your investing yourself.
You are the one who will have personally grown and become the master of *simple math*. You will have made it your lifelong friend, and companion and personal assistant.

Realize that distractions may be any person, place, or thing, or activity, or focus that pulls you away from doing and/or devoting your precious time to anything you chose to do in your best interest.
You must resist distractions and stay on course.

Work each problem by lifting the problem to your own page and review your calculations with the answer after working the problem, so that you are thinking through the ramifications of each problem.

Let's put on your thinking cap and get thinking and putting your determination into working the exercises. Doing so will be preparing you for developing your understanding and liking of *simple math* and how that leads to your graduation.

POEM TO READ DOWN, THEN UP

Perhaps you may think about math a certain way.
Let's turn that around.

Please Read Down, then Read Up -- and see yourself.

I am not a good person with math
So, do not try to convince me that
I am a very adept person with math
Because at the end of the day
I dislike myself in every single way
And I am not going to lie to myself by saying
There is potential inside of me that matters
So, rest assured I will remind myself
That I am a worthless, terrible person and poor at math
And nothing you say will make me believe
I still deserve to be recognized as a good person with math
Because no matter what
I am not good enough to be a good person with math
And I am in no position to believe that
Being a math person does exist within me
Because whenever I look in the mirror, I always think
Am I as poor with math as people say I am?

Do you see how you can turn thoughts around to be
positive thoughts when they may originate as negative?
Think about it.
Apply this to yourself and learning *simple math*.

SIMPLE MATH WORKBOOK
FOR ADULTS

This book offers an awakening of mind, body and spirit to the fun of *simple math*. It may trigger emotions and realizations of having almost been there. You are at a crossroads. It signals that you are here and there is time to correct your course when you make a conscious decision and take action to effect change and become a master of *simple math*. If anyone can learn this, you can. Put on your thinking cap, open your mind, and put your thoughts of other topics aside. Let the expectations you face be your own expectations, seen as self-challenges to be achieved by you.

This book will serve as a review and refresh for most readers.

CLASS IS IN SESSION

We will discuss with words and numbers so you may learn how it is to your great benefit that numbers and math are constants and logic in action. That way, and when you learn and befriend them, you will be prepared for them to serve your purposes.

Exercises offer you the opportunity to look at:

- Whole Numbers
- Count Up to 120 from 1
- Count Down from 120 to 1
- Count Money and Read Numbers
- Sidelight Lesson – Fuel Price
- Coronavirus; COVID-19 Pandemic – Read Numbers
- Addition
- Subtraction
- Addition – Subtraction Relationship Revealed in Proofs
- Proving Calculation
- Multiplication
- Shortcuts
- Times Tables
- Times Table Chart
- Division
- Multiplication – Division Relationship Revealed in Proofs
- Fractions – Proper and Improper
- Decimal Equivalents
- Decimal Equivalents Chart
- Averages, Estimates, Rounding, Ratios
- Reciprocals, Percentages,
- Fractions – Percentages Relationship Revealed in Proofs
- Measure
- Time Management
- Calendar
- Common Calculation Challenges
- The inter-relatedness of parts of math

- The Concepts of math
- Working Problems
- Discussions

You will learn about yourself and what you can do and what you need to work on to develop as a new habit. Decide before you do an exercise, that you will revisit the previous exercises for review and improve your performance to ready yourself for moving to a new exercise.

CONTRACT

When you make a contract with yourself, you commit to yourself that you choose the path of self-improvement. When you do this, you are acknowledging that you are consciously aware that you are making a choice to change. You understand that to create change, it is necessary to end a past way of thinking about something, responding to it or otherwise avoiding facing it, and working yourself through it to the other side of fear, or whatever holds you back. When you do this, you let go of the old in order to embrace, guide and fully experience your new A+ attitude, and new beginning. You may choose to carry this book as a quick-reference source, helping to keep you on course to your new beginning. You may choose to give this book to help another.

This is your Contract with Yourself.   Share it with your loved ones. They will be delighted to support you. You do this because you are committed to doing your best, learning and making yourself a master and friend of *Simple Math*.

_____   _____
  Name   Date

Copy and complete this Contract as a foundation for yourself.
Your commitment becomes real when you write it and share it.
Hang it on the wall as a reminder to yourself of this new goal.

EXERCISE ONE

Whole Numbers

Whole numbers are complete as you see and use them. There are no fractional parts of whole numbers. This exercise practices our use of whole numbers with the goal of understanding how they fit together and add up and down. You may have a tendency to speed through or even skip this or some exercises. That may prove to be a mistake. Allow yourself time to absorb the understanding you will gain in the hidden messages buried in each exercise. Visualize what you are learning. The goal of these exercises is more than having you memorize in order to do what is asked. Memory sharpens itself as you use it, and what you learn becomes a part of you. Yes, the goal is for you to become comfortable thinking about what you are doing and learning. Think about how each exercise builds on another and shows you how math comes together for you.

Dedicate and allow more time than you think you will need to do this and each exercise. Record your beginning and ending times. Then, calculate how long you worked on this exercise. Do the same the next time through and compare the elapsed times. When you do this, you are using *simple math* while learning it.

Also, think of what you are doing as you work your way up and down each series. Think about how you feel about what you may be learning about numbers and also about yourself. Remember, there are hidden benefits to repeating each exercise a number of times. When you advance beyond Exercise One, return and think and review what you learned here and how it has supported you in the next Exercises. When you do this with each completed exercise, you will do well for yourself.

It is recommended, and you may choose, to write the numbers and problems in each of these exercises down on your paper so that you can visualize them and see the relationship to the number to be able to get great value from this exercise. Doing this would be to your benefit. This is true whether you are on Kindle or reading paperback.

Think about what you are asked to do and do it.
This looks like a lot of work for you to do. It is.
This is what it takes for you to learn. So, dedicate yourself now.
You will get out of this course much more than you put into it.
Do well for yourself.

Recite the whole numbers up and down so you hear each number as you count. The exercise becomes more real and valuable when you speak, hear and see each number.

1-A Count Up to 120 aloud so you hear each number in sequence

   1, 2, 3, 4, 5 and on up to 120

1-B Count Down to 1 from 120 aloud

   120, 119, 118, and on down to 1

1-C Count Up to 120 by 2s aloud

   2, 4, 6, 8 and on up

1-D Count Down from 120 to zero by 2s aloud

   120, 118, 116 and on downward

1-E Count Up to 120 by 3s aloud

   3, 6, 9 and on up

1-F Count Down from 120 to zero by 3s aloud

   120, 117, 114, 111 and on down

1-G Count Up to 120 by 4s aloud

   4, 8, 12, 16 and on up

1-H   Count Down from 120 by 4s

120, 116, 112 and on down

1-I   Count Up to 120 by 5s aloud

5, 10, 15, 20, 25 and on up

1-J   Count Down from 120 by 5s

120, 115, 110 and on down

1-K   Count Up to 120 by 6s

6, 12, 18, 24, and on up

1-L   Count Down from 120 by 6s

120, 114, 108 and on down

1-M   Count Up to 140 by 7s

7, 14, 21 and on up

1-N   Count Down from 140 by 7s

140, 133, 126 and on down

1-O   Count Up to 96 by 8s

8, 16, 24 and on up

1-P   Count Down from 96 by 8s

96, 88, 80 and on down

1-Q   Count Up to 108 by 9s

9, 18, 27 and on up

1-R   Count Down from 108 by 9s

108, 99, 90 and on down

1-S   Count Up to 180 by 10s

10, 20, 30 and on up

1-T   Count Down from 180 by 10s

180, 170, 160 and on down

1-U   Count Up to 121 by 11s

11, 22, 33 and on up

1-V   Count Down from 121 by 11s

121, 110, 99 and on down

1-W Count Up to 120 by 12s

     12, 24, 36 and on up

1-X Count Down from 120 by 12s

     120, 108, 96 and on down

When you have repeated these aloud for several days,
then take a pad and pen and write each line out
all the way up and down again, as you first did this.

Then, look at the numbers running across your paper
and see how and where and why the numbers repeat
on the different lines.

Counting up from one shows you the simple way that
when you reach ten, the numbers repeat over ten and
count upward again by adding 1 through ten to the first digit
to the left and it keeps building higher numbers from Units to Tens to
the left to Hundreds to the left to Thousands further to the left.

When you really think clearly about these whole number sequences,
you may notice that you see buried in the sequence the multiplication of
numbers, as we will discuss later. You will see this when you write the
number sequence for each count line on the paper.

For example, you may see that counting to 120 by 2s is really writing
the multiples of two upward in the sequence. This shows the constancy
and logic in math.

Even numbers (2, 4, 6 on up) repeat in the far-right position up to ten
Odd numbers (1, 3, 5, 7 on up) also repeat in the far-right position up to nine
Two-digit numbers add to the left beginning with 10
Three-digit numbers add to the left beginning with 100
Four-digit numbers add to the left beginning with 1,000
These are all whole numbers because there are no fractional values. We understand that these numbers may have a decimal to the right. We need not write the decimal because they are whole numbers with no fractional amount to be shown after the decimal.

An example of that would be $1.33 being one dollar and thirty-three cents as the .33 showing that there is a fractional amount in the number.

Figure out the relationships and why this happens.
Think about this until understanding comes through.

Write on your pad of paper your own thoughts about what you see in the numbers. When we write what we think, it helps clarify and solidify our understanding.

Continue to practice speaking and writing the process in Exercise One.

When we look at whole numbers, there are values to each number in the larger number. They are known as place value number assignments based on where the digit is in a number series.
They begin on the right and move leftward as the numbers rise in power.

COUNT MONEY and READ NUMBERS

When we count money, we count in whole numbers, then Units and Tens and Hundreds. Practice counting and see the combinations available when counting coins to add to a certain amount.
We count the whole number amounts before we count fractional amounts after the decimal. Remember, after the decimal means that the numbers to the right of the decimal are fractional and less than 1.

We normally count the largest currency bills first and work downward to the smaller denominations. We do the same with coins. When we do this, we are counting the whole number values first and then adding the fractional values numbers to the sum of the whole numbers.

Let's say we are counting cash in a cash drawer at work. We begin by adding up the100 dollar bills first; next, we add the 50 dollar bills to the sum of the 100 dollar bills. Then, we add the 20 dollar bills and add the sum to the total of the $100 and the $50. Then, we add the ten dollar bills and add the sum to the total of the $100 plus the $50 and arrive at a new Total. Then we do the same with the $5 and $1 bills and arrive at a new Grand Total of currency cash.

We add coins the same. We begin with $0.50; next with $0.25; next with $0.10 and next with $0.05 and finally with the $0.01 copper cent. When we do this, we accumulate the value upward until we determine the value of all the coins and arrive at a new Grand Total of coins cash.

Units

We always begin on the right.
The first digit on the right is the ones place or the Units place.
That would be the same as a penny in a dollar because 100 cents = $1.00   One penny more shows as $1.01.   The $0.01 is one cent.
One cent is one Unit. Ten of them makes ten cents or a dime. The ten cents space moves left into the second column. Ten X $0.10 = 1.00.

Tens

The next place (second digit) to the left is the Tens place.
That is where the $0.10 (ten-cents) lives.
That is ten one-hundreds of one dollar or ten cents.
It takes ten of these to make 100 cents or one dollar.

If we had a fraction, as discussed later, it would show 10/100.
We reduced that to be 1/10 because we know that there are ten 10s in 100. So, we also know there are 20 10s in 200 and 30 tens in 300.

Remember that when we counted by ten, the Units place had numbers 0, 1, 2, 3, 4, 5, 6, 7, 8 through 9. When we count higher than 9, the Units place on the right becomes zero and the tens place next to the decimal becomes 1 because we add 1 to the left as the numbers amount rise. With the Units place at zero, it reads .10 and then we begin rising numbers in the Units place again from 0 to 9 before the 9 again becomes zero and we add one to the Tens column number and it would become .20 and then again the numbers rise and arrive at .30, .40, .50, .60, .70, .80, and .90 (like 90 pennies or 90 cents in one dollar) after which ten more makes a whole one dollar $1.00, with both the Units and Tens places to the right of the decimal being zeroes signifying that there are no fractional parts in this number. The $1 became a whole number.

Yes, the Tens position is like 10 cents ($0.10) to 90 cents ($0.90) in a dollar.
Whatever the number is, it is multiplied by ten to determine its value.

Hundreds
The third place to the left is Hundreds. The number is multiplied by one-hundred to determine its value. This is where we get $1.00.
It represents 100 pennies or 100 one-cents. We just counted up to this position and it became itself when the Tens space reached 99 and then one more was added. $99 + 1 = 100$ The 1 in the 100 is in the hundreds position.

INTERESTING SIDLIGHT LESSON – FUEL PRICE

There is something we see hidden in the price of a gallon of gas.
There is a third digit to the right of the decimal. It is 9.
It is to the right of the Units-position, where we would think there would be no number.
Yet, we see a gas- station gallon price may be $3.729.
We understand that it is 9/10 of a penny more than $3.72.
[.009 X 100 = 0.9]
That is 9/10 of a cent or 1/10 less than one penny.
What is happening is that almost one additional cent is being squeezed into the cost of a gallon of gas. Most people may not realize this.

The price range of gas is $3.729 to $4.17 and in 2022 even up to $5 per gallon regular gas as a result of global economic distress and price increases due to the Russian invasion of Ukraine February 24, 2022.

The importance of this is what it does for the fuel companies.
An average of 338 million gallons of gas are sold in the US daily.
That 9/10 of a cent hidden in the price of a gallon of gas multiplied by the record of 338,000,000 gallons = $3,042,000 [Three million, forty-two thousand dollars] additional revenue daily to fuel companies by adding the 9/10 of a cent to each gallon.
Think about this when you see prices.

Thousands

The fourth place to the left is Thousands. The number is multiplied by a number from one to ten to determine its value as $1,000.00.

We place a comma to the left of the third digit from the decimal.

$1,000.00 One-thousand dollars (and no cents) or $1,000 whole number

Ten-thousands
The fifth place to the left is Ten-thousands. The number is multiplied by a number from one to ten to determine its value.

We place a comma to the left of the third digit from the decimal.

$10,000.00 Ten-thousand dollars (and no cents) $10,000

One-hundred-thousands
The sixth place to the left is one-hundred-thousands. The number is multiplied by a number from one to ten to determine its value.

$100,000.00   One-hundred-thousand dollars (and no cents)

Again, we place a comma to the left of the third digit from the decimal.

Given that there are no cents, the numbers are often written as whole numbers without the decimal and zeroes in the tens and units positions. Either way would be acceptable.

See and understand how the numbers accumulate and rise to higher numbers. We may automatically add each day, and not know this.

Millions

The seventh place to the left is Millions. The number is multiplied by a number from one to ten to determine its value.

$1,000,000.00   One-million Dollars (and no cents) $1,000,000

One million has six zeroes.

We place a comma to the left of the third digit and the sixth digit.

$1,222,333.44   One million, two-hundred twenty-two thousand, three-hundred thirty-three Dollars and forty-four cents.

$11,222,333.44   Eleven million, two-hundred twenty-two thousand, three-hundred thirty-three Dollars and forty-four cents.

These numbers and place values continue to rise as far as you would like to go.

We can stop here. You probably may not deal with higher numbers. We do know that astronomers and NASA people and government reporters deal with higher numbers because they report great distances in outer-space or about the government budget and costs of operation.

Coronavirus Pandemic

Now, we know that the COVID-19 United States Deaths have risen to a number reported to be 834,455 Total Deaths in the United States. Read the number as (834) eight hundred thirty-four thousand then (455) four-hundred fifty five Total Deaths. See the place value of the digits and the comma in this whole number.

The Total Cases are 52,788,451. Read the number as (52) fifty-two million (millions are the next place values to the left higher than hundred-thousands) then (788) seven-hundred eighty-eight thousand then (451) four-hundred fifty-one Total Cases in the United States on Friday December 24, 2021.

You need to know how to read these numbers and what the size of the number means.

As these numbers increase, the added amounts are added on the right column and build up higher above ten and then add to the Tens column next and then spill over to the Hundreds column next and then to the Thousands column next and then to the Ten-thousands column next and then to the Hundred-thousand column next and then to the Millions column next and then expand to the Ten-millions column next and then to the Hundred-millions column next and then to the Ten-hundred-million or the Billions column next and onward.

COVID-19

We see the rise in the numbers of COVID-19 Total Cases World-wide reaching 611,610,134 on September 7, 2022.
Read this number as (611) six-hundred eleven million, then (610) six-hundred-ten thousand, then (134) one-hundred-thirty-four cases of persons world-wide who have COVID-19 basic or its Delta Variant or its Omicron Variant as of Wednesday September 7, 2022.
The numbers continue to rise and be noteworthy.
An Exercise Five challenge addresses this for you.
Below is a link that would bring you up-to-date on COVID-19 Cases.

https://www.google.com/search?client=firefox-b-1-d&q=covid-19+statistics+worldwide

That will be a picture of what we will get into later on to see how large the US numbers are as a portion of the World numbers of cases and deaths so far. Also, later and on your own you may wish to research and compare the statistics of other countries with the US numbers and see how the US fares compared to them.

COVID-19 Coronavirus Pandemic Update October 20, 2022

Global		
Total Cases	631,722,073	100%
Recovered	610,609,176	
Deaths	6,577,917	
Infected Today	14,534,980	

United States		
Total Cases	98,987,014	100%
Recovered	96,335,228	
Deaths	1,092,031	
Infected Today	1,559,755	

Calculate the percentages of 100% for each line after you work problems of percentages later on.

It is important that you know that the Coronavirus COVID-19, and its Omicron Variants continue to ravage the population in 228 countries.

EXERCISE TWO

2-A   Addition

Addition accumulates two or more numbers. Addition adds one number to another number. See the relationship of the numbers. See objects representing the numbers. The plus sign {+} is symbol for add.

$1 + 1 = 2$
$2 + 2 = 4$
$3 + 2 = 5$
$2 + 4 = 6$
$3 + 4 = 7$
$1 + 2 = 3$

$10 + 20 = 30$
See what we did. We added the numbers in each column across
From right to left.
$0 + 0 = 0$ $1 + 2 = 3$ $10 + 20 = 30$
$30 + 5 = 35$
This time we add $0 + 5 = 5$ $3 + 0 + 3$ answer is 35

Add downward:
30
+5
35

  30
+ 30
  60

When we add a group of numbers, we add by column to the right and moving left. As we add, when a number equals 10 or greater, we enter the right digit in the answer line and add the left digit (1) to the left as it is greater than nine and therefore raises the next number to the left by one. That is known as carrying one over to the next number to be added in.

```
   36269
+  15678
   51947
```

$9 + 8 = 17$ so, we enter the **7** under the column and since the number 17 is 10 or greater, we add (carry over) 1 to the column to the left. That number is called a carry-over that gets added to the number to the left.
(Later, we will learn in Subtraction that we do the opposite by borrowing ten as one from the number on the left and that reduces that number by one.)
So, the next column to the left becomes $1 + 6 + 7 = 14$ so, we enter **4** under the column added and since 14 is 10 or greater, we add 1 to the column to the left.
So, the next column to the left becomes $1 + 2 + 6 = 9$ so, we enter **9** under the column added and since 9 is less than ten, we have no 1 to add to the column to the left.
$6 + 5 = 11$ So, we enter **1** under the column added and since 11 is 10 or greater, we add 1 to the column to the left. If there is no column to the left, we bring the full number down as part of the answer.
$1 + 3 + 1 = 5$ So, we bring down the number **5** under the column added.
The answer is: **51947**

Think about what we just did. When we add, we are accumulating more of something. So, the numbers must rise just as when you were calling out rising numbers in Exercise One. Likewise, when you were calling out declining numbers, that was like subtracting, because the numbers were becoming less. We will see the subtracting later.

CALCULATION PROOF

Later, when we discuss that you can come back to this problem and subtract the second row from the answer row and arrive at the number on the top row. You can also subtract the answer row from the top row and arrive at the second-row number. We call this calculation a way of proving your answer is correct. With numbers, there are ways to prove an answer because numbers are constant.

~~~~~~~~~~~~

We can take any number at random and dissect it and see what makes it up.

We can work these numbers around and visualize and see that as we accumulate different sets of these same numbers, they all prove themselves.

So, we see that 7 equals a combination of 6 + 1, 5 + 2, 4 + 3, or 3 +4, 2 + 5, or 1 + 6 or 7 + 0.

SUGGESTION

Mental gymnastics suggest that when you are walking around seeing whatever in your life or sitting idle resting, thoughtfully look at what you see rather than turn to social media input to consume your time. Look at relationships to find similarities and dis-similarities and count them and compare them. They may be windows in a building, door handles, squares in carpeting, ceiling tiles, ceiling lights, pictures on the walls, people in the room or whatever. Count what you see and work the basic count of numbers forward and backward to strengthen your observation skills as well as to play the numbers in your mind.

When you may be walking or biking, think of what you see. Put aside the music of the world and let the beauty of the world in the sights before you become more-real than they would otherwise be if you were merely passing through. Become consciously aware of what you see and where you are. When you play the math game in your mind, you will find that this fits in and you may even find a hidden part of yourself stimulated by the new-world-experience you may be giving yourself. When you do this, you enhance your life.
Math leads you to appreciate more than just the little addition, or other numbers, you may be working with.

Work numbers up and down. Add this number to that number. Add another number to that answer.   Practice makes improvement and sets you up with a good foundation on which higher math may be built. Be sure to add as you see something. When you see a license plate on a vehicle, add the numbers up and experience the fun.

When you are with friends, think about or try talking about how to add numbers and work through fun calculations as an alternative to sitting idly on a cell phone on social media possibly giving away your valuable hours.

When you engage others, the social aspect of being together is more real when the conversation includes fun with math as an alternative to other pursuits. Add away and keep on adding.

Remember to visualize the problem. Visualizing leads you to answers.

2-B   Subtraction

Subtraction takes a number or quantity from another.
It is the opposite of addition.
In our addition example, we added numbers to equal seven.
In subtraction we take a number away to get a lesser number, known
as the difference.

The symbol {-} minus is take-away in subtraction.

In conversation, we say "what is the difference?" That expression
is an expression of thinking of subtraction. We can say that:
If you had seven bananas and remove one, you would have six.
Six is the difference.

Following this sequence down we find:
7-1 = 6 as the difference
7-2 = 5
7-3 = 4
7-4 = 3
7-5 = 2
See the relationship?

Numbers are constants. That is why *simple math* is learnable for you.

REAL-LIFE PRACTICE

Count the trees in the park when you are sitting there. Look around in a circle and count every tree you can see. Let's say 10 trees total. Write down the number of trees. 10 trees. Total.

Then, count trees without turning your head. 4 trees. Write that number below the first number of total trees. 4 trees. To take away.

Subtract or take away the number of trees you counted in your more-narrow focus.
The answer is the number of trees you cannot see without turning your head.
You quickly know the answer in your mind without thinking about it.

The answer number is known as the *difference*.
```
 10   trees
 -4   trees take away (trees easily seen)
  6   trees is the number difference – the number of trees not seen
```

When we add the difference (trees not seen) to the number of trees seen,
We arrive at the total trees. That is addition. Addition is the opposite of subtraction. Addition can be used to prove subtraction because it is the opposite of subtraction.

Room holds 63 people seated, though 13 are standing,
16 people sit at 2 tables
8 people are sitting in chairs directly under 8 spotlights
6 chairs by the wall are empty

Decide which information given applies to the problem

Calculate the number of additional chairs needed

$63 - 16 - 8 - 6 =$

CALCULATE PURCHASE

Purchases of items paid by cash uses dollars of different values or denominations. When we handle money (dollar bills and coins) we add and subtract to exchange money for the valued items purchased.

Purchase value of $32.75
We may pay by offering:
32 single dollar bills + change of three quarters
6 $5 bills plus 2 singles plus 3 quarters or other change equal to $0.75
1 $20 plus 1 $10 plus 2 singles and change
You get the point.

Or, payment could be a total of $33 cash, however denominated, with the expected return of a quarter or 2 dimes and one nickel.

Many people do these simple math calculations without thinking deeply.

This is how you may develop your *simple math* skills.

The above is basic addition to the purchase value or subtraction of the purchase value from a higher amount of money presented for payment.

When we subtract large numbers, we write the smaller below the other and subtract by beginning at the right column and doing a take away. If we have to borrow a number from the column left top line because that number is smaller than the (digit) number being subtracted, that top line number to the left becomes progressively lower by one each time we borrow, as we continue moving left in our take-aways until we get to the far-left column.

```
  664729
- 462731
  201998
```

We subtract the lower number from the upper number in each column.
9 take away 1 = 8 So, we enter number **8** below the column
We cannot take 3 from 2. So, we borrow 1 (actually ten) from the 7 to the left making it now six. The 1 becomes 10 when we borrow it.
So, then we have {10 + 2} 12 from which to subtract 3.
12 – 3 = 9 So, we enter **9** under the column we are working with
It is then the second digit from the right in the answer

We then move left and subtract 7 from 6. We cannot. So, we borrow 1 from the 4 which becomes 3 and the 6 becomes 16 when the one becomes ten because it would be in the left digit of two in our column.
6 + 10 = 16 top line of the column
16 - 7 = **9** which we enter under the column we are working with as the third digit from the right in the answer
Next, we subtract 2 from 3 (we borrowed one from the 4)
3 – 2 = **1** which we enter under the column we are working with as
The fourth digit from the right in the answer
Next, we move left and subtract 6 from 6 = **0** and enter zero in the answer as the fifth digit from the right.
Next, we move left and subtract 4 from 6 = 2 and enter **2** in the answer as the sixth digit from the right.
We see our answer (the difference between the two numbers) arrived at by subtraction is **201998**.

PROVING CALCULATION

As discussed at the end of addition, the answer (difference) in this problem may be proved by adding upward 201998 plus 462731 to arrive at 664729.
Another double check proof is to take away or subtract the 201998 from 664729 to arrive at 462731.
Work these to see how easy this comes together for you to understand.

Because numbers are constant, proofs work out and balance to correct calculations. If a proof fails, then you know there is a mistake in the calculation to be researched and resolved.

Practice makes improvement and understanding.
Practice subtracting large numbers so the process becomes understood. The principles of subtraction become easier to understand as you practice against real-life situation numbers.

Practice, as though you were a cashier, giving change for a $1.00 bill

Practice as though you were a cashier giving change to a customer who hands you $1.37 for a $1.32 purchase. You received a quarter, a dime and two pennies. You may wonder why you received too much change. The reason is because the change you would give back is $0.05, a nickel. The customer calculated in thought and decided to unload coins in the pocket. It could be that the customer had the quarter and dime and two cents and was unable to give exact change while giving close change. So, the nickel you return is one-half of the dime you received. Focus and think because you have to be able to see the entire transaction.

Begin your practice with small numbers and see how they relate. You may enjoy these exercises and be able to help others understand math and how to subtract numbers. When you discuss and help others with math, you cement the lessons and techniques you learned.

Now, we will look at subtracting large numbers.

      1,977,924 One million, nine hundred seventy-seven thousand, nine hundred twenty-four

 less <u>1,615,629</u> One million, six hundred fifteen thousand, six hundred twenty-nine

      362,295 Difference is three hundred sixty-two thousand, two hundred ninety-five

First, read the problem aloud. Read the words and see them in the numbers.

There is a decimal understood to be to the right.
Because these are whole numbers, the decimal is not needed.

First comma from the right in number: ,924 means Hundreds
Second comma to the left in number: ,977 means Thousands
Number to the left of second comma means Millions

This was discussed under whole numbers in Exercise One.

To subtract:

```
   1,977,924
-  1,615,629
     362,295
```

Always begin on right.
We cannot take 9 from 4. So, we borrow 1 from the 2 on the left. That makes the 2 a 1 on the left. The borrow (remember when we borrow 1 that it is really ten) makes the 4 a number 14.
9 from 14 = 5, which we enter beginning from the right and under the 9 as the first digit in our answer known as the difference.
Second column to the left: we cannot take 2 from 1 above. Remember that we took 1 from the column 2 #2 and made the column 1 on right 14. So, we again take 1 from the top left next number (9) and it becomes 8. So, now we have 11 in the second column from the right.
2 from 11 = 9, which we enter beginning from the right and under the 2 in second column.
Third column to the left: Top number 9 is now 8 because we took one. So, 6 from 8 = 2, which we enter beginning from the right and under the 6 in third column.
Fourth column to the left: Top number 7 remains a whole number 7 because nothing was borrowed from it.
5 from 7 = 2, which we enter beginning from the right and under the 5 in fourth column.
Fifth column to the left: 1 from 7 = 6, entered below the 1.
Sixth column to the left: 6 from 9 = 3, entered below the 6.
Seventh column to the left: 1 from 1 = 0 so no entry below.
Difference is 362,295 read as three hundred sixty-two thousand, two hundred ninety-five.

We can prove the answer by adding vertically and carry over a 1 to the column on the left when the number becomes ten or more.
So, 5 + 9 =14 carry 1 to the left
Column two: 9 + 2 = 11 + 1 carry over = 12 so we post the 2 and carry over the 1 to next column to left
Column three: 2 + 6 = 8 + 1 carry over = 9
Column four: 2 + 5 = 7
Column five: 6 + 1 = 7
Column six: 3 + 6 = 9
Column seven: zero plus 1 = 1

Proof works for us.

Let's go further using the number we calculated to be the Difference.

Read these numbers aloud and then look at the text to be sure
you are reading the amounts correctly.

	362,295	three hundred sixty-two thousand, two hundred ninety-five
Minus	171,507	one hundred seventy-one thousand, five hundred seven
	190,788	one hundred ninety thousand, seven hundred eighty-eight

Work this one out yourself.
The 5 has to borrow or take 1 from the 9. So, the 9 becomes ____
The 2 has to borrow or take 1 from the 2. So, the 2 becomes ____
The 6 has to borrow or take 1 from the 3. So, the 3 becomes ____

Prove your answer by adding upward.

Now you see how adding and subtracting are related opposites.
That is why it is easy to prove the calculations.
Daily practice leads to improvement and understanding.

8, 1, 2

EXERCISE THREE

3-A   Multiplication

Multiplication is as simple as addition.
IT IS.

It is a shortcut to the same answer as in addition.

The symbol {X} means multiply.

We know, without thinking, that 5 $1 bills are equal to $5.

We talked about how numbers play an important part in life.
Few things or experiences are singular.
Most things or experiences appear in multiples.

Life is an accumulation of items and experiences flashing before us.
Focus your attention on the frequency of appearances of commonalities
and differences.
Multiply those out.
How?
Watch for and identify opportunities to work simple numbers in your
mind. Then, focus on doing this instead of looking for entertainment or
other distractions.

You can take any number and add it or instead multiply it like this:

We have two peaches   2
If we say 2 peaches in each of two baskets is:
Two peaches X two baskets or 2 x 2 = 4 peaches
That is a multiplication shortcut to saying we have 2 peaches each in 2 peaches baskets = 4 peaches
This is a shortcut to thinking 2 peaches + 2 peaches = 4 peaches

This applies if we use large numbers:
20 peaches: is 2 peaches x 10 = 20 peaches
(Remember we discussed the place value of a number in whole numbers in Exercise One)
What we did is just add a zero to multiply by ten based on the place value.
2 peaches x 10 = 20 peaches   2 X 1 = 2 and add or bring down the zero
The long way of saying it is 2 peaches x 0 = 0 peaches in the Units place value
2 peaches x 1 = 2 peaches in the Tens place value
Then we add the number 2 in the Tens place and the 0 in the Units place value. That gives us 20.

Multiplication Shortcuts to practice and understand:

Add a zero to a number and it is multiplied by ten.
That is because it moves it to the place value of Tens. 10
1 X 10 = 10

Add two zeroes to a number and it is multiplied by one hundred.
That is because it moves the number to the place value of Hundreds.
100 1 X 100 = 100

Add three zeroes to a number and it is multiplied by one thousand.
That is because it moves the number to the place value of Thousands.
1,000   1 X 1,000 = 1,000   These are all whole numbers.

When we get to review division, you will see that division is the opposite
of multiplication.

To multiply a number: let's say 2,000

By 10 you can add a zero and 2,000 becomes 20,000

Shortcut:
By 20 you can add two zeroes and divide by 5
2,000 X 20 = 40,000
2,000 + 2 zeroes = 200,000 divided by 5 = 40,000

We can do this because adding 2 zeroes makes it like 100 as we just
learned in the Multiplication Shortcuts above.
Then, because we know that there are 5 20s in 100 (5 X 20 = 100),
after we make the number Hundreds by adding the two zeroes, then we
can simply divide by the 5 (5 20 s in 100) and arrive at our answer.

The same shortcut is shown below for other numbers because the
same formula is a constant in all numbers.
See below:

Multiply by 25 - you can add two zeroes and divide by 4 because there are 4 25s in 100.

We know there are 4 quarters in a dollar. That is the same.
When you add the two zeroes, you added one-hundred.
So, then you divide by 4 and quickly get your answer.
We just talked about this above.
That is the shortcut.

This is the long calculation:

```
    2,000      Two thousand
    X  25      Twenty five
   10,000      Ten thousand
Add 4000       Four thousand
   50,000      Fifty thousand
```
Or
2000 plus 2 zeroes = 200,000   Two hundred thousand
How many 4 are in 200,000?
Answer is 50,000
Ask yourself how many times 4 goes into 20
That leads you to see the answer
Work it out to be sure you begin to see what we are learning

Multiply by 50 - you can add two zeroes and divide by 2 because there are 2 50s in the 100 you just added as 100 to use the shortcut

47 X 50 = 2350

[What I would do with this is quickly see that the answer will be one-half of 47, which would be 23 plus a fraction because 2 X 23 = 46.
So, there is a remainder of 1 of which half is in the answer. So, 23.5 x 2 = 47]   This is the type calculation you do in your head.

47 place decimal and add 2 zeroes = 47.00

  _23.50   twenty-three and one-half   or 23 1/2
2) 47.00
   4
  07
   6
  10
  10

Proof: 2 X 23.50 = 4700

23.50
X 2
4700
 2 X 0 = 0 enter 0; 2 X 5 = 10 enter 0 and carry 1 to left
 2 X 3 = 6 + the 1 carried = 7
 2 X 2 = 4

Below is a long multiplication calculation.

    2,000 Two thousand
     X 50   Fifty
  100,000   One-hundred-thousand
Same result

Multiply large numbers
Begin on right and enter answer to left beginning below multiplier
Then add vertically

735 X 152826:

You will multiply 152826 735 times. Multiplication is the shortcut to listing 152826 vertically 735 times and then adding the column of the same number manually to arrive at the answer.

```
    152826 Multiplier is the number being multiplied
  X    735 Multiplicand is the number times the multiplier
    764130      Product #1
    458478      Product #2
  1069782       Product #3
  112327110 Answer is labeled Product (add the 3 Products)
```

    112,327,110   When we place the comma each three digits to the left, we read the number as:

One hundred twelve million, three hundred twenty-seven thousand, One hundred ten

You will note that we caried amounts to the left when above 9 in the Tens column. Such as: 5 x 6 = 30 so, bring down the **0** and carry the three to be added to the left. 5 x 2 = 10 and add the 3 for 13. So, bring down the **3** and carry the one to the left. 5 x 8 =40 and add the one for 41. Bring down the **one** and carry the 4 to the left. 5 x 2 = 10 and add the 4 carried to the left for 14. Bring down the **4** and carry the 1 to the left. 5 x 5 = 25 plus the one carried to the left = 26. Bring down the **6** and carry the 2 to the left. 5 x 1 = 5 and add the 2 caried over for 5+2=**7**.   So, we see that 5 X 152826 = 764130
Multiply by the 3 and the 7 as illustrated to arrive at your answer.

Multiply by 75 - you can

    2,000 Two thousand
    <u>X 75</u>   Seventy five
  150,000   One hundred fifty-thousand

Notice that if you dropped zeroes and saw this problem as
2 times 75
you may quickly see that it is the same as
2 times two sets of (3 quarters or 75 cents) that equal $1.50.
When you see this in your mind, then you may see moving the decimal
two places to the right and adding back the three zeroes would make
sense as the answer is merely a multiple of the simple calculation.
Yes, it will take a while for some to see this shortcut.

When you learn how to think the shortcuts in math, you may see that
they give you enough quick calculation to make an estimate or to
approximate the outcome of a calculation on paper or to see the
reasonableness of the number you arrive at.

Practice these shortcuts to math at every opportunity.

A 9-story building has 12 windows on each side of each floor
Each window has 4 section panes
Calculate the number of panes of glass on each floor
Calculate the number of panes of glass on one entire side
of the building
Calculate the number of panes of glass on entire building

12w x 4s x 4p = 192
12w x 4p = 48
12w x 4p x 4s x 9f = 1728

 Proof: 192 x 9 = 1728
          48 x 4 = 1728

~~~~~~~~~~~~~~

Airplane carries 247 paying passengers along with 6 flight attendants.
Each person is allowed two pieces of luggage weighing 40-pounds or
less.
Calculate the maximum total luggage weight.
10,120

Each month you will pay S $0.90

Each month you will pay T $9.00

Each month you will pay U $90.00

Each month you will pay V $900.00

Each month you will pay W $9,000.00

Each month you will pay X $9,134.56

Each month you will pay Y $91,345.67

Each month you will pay Z $13.27

Calculate the total you will pay in one year at each monthly rate:

Calculate the total you will pay in one year to all parties:

Calculate the average amount paid monthly over the term:
          (Averages are discussed in Exercise Four)
S $10.80   T $108   U $1,080   V $10,800   W $108,000
X $109,614.72   Y $1,096,148.04   Z $159.24 $1,325,920.80/12
Average $110,493.40

3-B Times Tables

Times Tables are to be learned and thought about for days for understanding. When you learn and understand the tables, then you need not memorize them. You will just end up knowing the answers without memorization. That is when times tables have become one with your math thought process.

Look over the table below and see its pattern and the constants. See how the numbers flow and make sense. Remember the Exercise One sequences when you went up and down the various whole numbers to speak and visualize and understand the relationships and sequences.

The logic of multiplication is simple because the principle is fixed. Multiplication is the opposite of division, which we will later discuss. The logic of division is simple because the principle is fixed. These two opposite calculations prove each other just the same as we learned that addition and subtraction prove each other.

You can look at the times table we just discussed and see multiplication. Later you will see division is the opposite of the multiplication number on the Times Table. The diagonal line from 1 downward to 12 in the lower right corner is there for a reason. It shows two numbers of the same value multiplied by themselves. It also leads you to see division as the opposite.

The chart below goes up to 12. Challenge yourself to write or construct and continue the chart up to 20. You will learn much by accepting this challenge. Your gift of that educational experience will last and serve you for your lifetime.

Teach yourself this chart by studying it to fully understand it. Work the numbers backward and forward so you see multiplication and division at play in the chart.

Times Table Chart

--

X	0	1	2	3	4	5	6	7	8	9	10	11	12
0	0	0	0	0	0	0	0	0	0	0	0	0	0
1	0	1	2	3	4	5	6	7	8	9	10	11	12
2	0	2	4	6	8	10	12	14	16	18	20	22	24
3	0	3	6	9	12	15	18	21	24	27	30	33	36
4	0	4	8	12	16	20	24	28	32	36	40	44	48
5	0	5	10	15	20	25	30	35	40	45	50	55	60
6	0	6	12	18	24	30	36	42	48	54	60	66	72
7	0	7	14	21	28	35	42	49	56	63	70	77	84
8	0	8	16	24	32	40	48	56	64	72	80	88	96
9	0	9	18	27	36	45	54	63	72	81	90	99	108
10	0	10	20	30	40	50	60	70	80	90	100	110	120
11	0	11	22	33	44	55	66	77	88	99	110	121	132
12	0	12	24	36	48	60	72	84	96	108	120	132	144

--

Times Table Chart

3-C   Division

We learned the logic of multiplication is simple because the principle is fixed.
The logic of division is simple because the principle is fixed.
Division is the opposite of multiplication, we just discussed.
They prove each other just the same as we learned that addition and subtraction prove each other.

The symbol for division:
    . dot
    - hyphen
    . dot

You can look at the times table we just discussed and see division as the opposite of the multiplication number.
The diagonal line from 1 downward to 12 in the lower right corner is there for a reason. It shows two numbers of the same value multiplied by themselves. It also leads you to see division as the opposite.

Look at number 2 on the Times Table Chart.
You see that 2 X 2 = 4 in the diagonal line signaling the multiplication of the same number.
Well, when you look at the 4 and see the number 2 in the adjacent related boxes, you can see that 4 divided by 2 = 2.
This is an example of a proof.
Likewise, as you go down the line, you can see that 64 divided by 8 = 8
And 144 divided by 12 = 12. Pick each number and see how this process fits.

Example: If each of you had 2 applies, you have 4 apples among yourselves. See that 2 X 2 = 4.
See that the other side of that equation is 4 divided by either 2 = 2
Think about how this works anywhere on the Times Table.

Take a number and divide it by 2 and it is half as much or 50%. We will discuss percentages later. Percentage is noted here because it is a common term you are familiar with.

Take a number and divide it by 4 and it is 25% of what it was because 4 X 25 = 100
Any number arrived at by dividing by 4 will always be 25%.

Whatever the number is that we take to break apart, the number is 100% before we divide because it is whole.
A US $1.00 bill is 100% because it is whole.
When we take a part of the $1.00 bill, we identify the part as a part of the whole. So, we know that the part is a percentage of the whole $1.

A US $1.25 is 100% because it is whole as a dollar and a quarter ($0.25) while also being fractional because of the .25
When we break it apart in it largest pieces, we know it is a $1 plus twenty-five cents or ($0.25) – a quarter, which is 1/4 of 1.
The two pieces apart still equal the whole $1.25.

~~~~~

We have a whole pie. It is 100% complete.
We cut the pie into 4 pieces.
Each piece is one-quarter of the pie.
We see this similar to the dollar example.
Four quarters of pie equals the whole pie just the same as four quarters ($0.25) we know equals a whole dollar.
So, we see that we divide a whole and it always equals the sum of its parts.

We are in a group of 15 persons going on a 15-mile hike.
We expect to walk 2.5 miles-per-hour or less depending on terrain and stops for scenery and rest breaks.
As we walk farther, we may become more tired and walk slower.
Besides the 10-pounds we can have in our backpacks, each of us will carry an allocated group-assigned-amount of baggage weight.
The total group weight to be allocated is 177 pounds.
Calculate the additional weight each hiker will carry.
Calculate the total weight each hiker will carry.
Calculate how long we will be away if the average speed is 2 MPH.

Divide 177 by 15 and round your answer:

         _11_____ each person caried extra 11 pounds +
15 persons) 177 pounds
       15
        27
        15
        12 remainder is fraction 12/15

Divide 12 by 15

  __ 0___
15) 12
        So, we add decimal and two zeroes

   0.80   8 X 15 = 120
15) 12.00   how many times does 15 go into 120?
            How many 15s are in 120?
We know that 6 X 15 = 90 and 90 is 30 less than 120
We know that 30 is twice (or 2X) 15
So, it appears that 8 X 15 might be 120.
So, we divided and confirmed this number.
0.80 is the same as 80 cents in a dollar

We move the decimal two places to the right and convert
 a decimal to a percentage
Two decimal places equal 100
(Remember that $1.00 is 100 pennies)
So, we move the decimal and add the percent sign and see that our
percentage is 80%
The problem asked us to round up or down for the answer.
Because 80% is greater than 50% (or one-half or ½) we round up for
your answer.

State the number of allocated pounds each hiker will carry _____
Calculate the total weight each hiker will carry _____
Calculate Total Hike Time at 2 MPH hike speed_____
Remember that Distance = Rate X Time
Time = Distance divided by Rate

11 pounds extra

11 + 10 =

Distance = Rate or Speed times [X} Time
D = R x T

15 divided by 2 MPH =

_____
2) 15

2 is a whole number and 15 is a whole number

Division asks how many 2s are in 15?
We know that 2 X 7 = 14

So, first digit in quotient is 7 with a remainder of 1

We place the remainder of 1 over the 2 for a fraction 1/2
We know that ½ is 50% or like half-dollar or .50
So, we know our quotient (result or answer) is going to be:

7.5 the same as 71/2

Airplane carries 247 paying passengers along with 6 flight attendants.
Each person is allowed and has two pieces of luggage.
Total weight of luggage in the cargo bay is 20,240

Calculate the maximum total luggage pieces allowed for each person
on board. Understand what the words tell you.
Calculate the average luggage weight per bag.

247 + 6 =
253 x 2 =

Which number divides into _____) 20,240

80

MILES PER GALLON

We move and use various forms of transportation. When you are in a
vehicle, it is important that you know about the capacity of your fuel tank
and how to read the gauge so you may be able to know the fuel
remaining in the tank and whether it is enough to get you to your
destination and return. When you know these numbers, you may be
able to calculate or estimate the numbers. Some people run out of gas
because they might not look at the gauge or just do not think about this
until it is too late. Be sure that you now know to read the gauge. When
you know the maximum fill of the gas tank is 16 gallons, then you know
that when the gauge shows 3/4, there would be about 12 gallons in the
tank. If the gauge shows 1/2, you would know there would be about 8
gallons in the tank. If the gauge shows 1/4, you would know there would
be about 4 gallons in the tank.

Now, this information is important when you can link it to the distance
the vehicle can go on one gallon of gas. That is known as Miles Per
Gallon. Remember that miles-per-gallon varies depending on driving
pattern, temperature, efficiency of engine, proper maintenance, flow-
driving instead of stop-and-go city driving, idling the vehicle, use of

heater or air conditioning drawing down engine power, and other variables.

Let's say for this discussion that we determine that the car will consume one gallon of gas for every 25 miles distance it covers.
So, a 16-gallon fuel tank X 25 miles per gallon = 400 miles may be the expected distance range, on average, you may expect to cover on a tank of gas. This calculation really comes into play when you would be traveling distances, such as between cities.

Now, how do you determine the recent miles-per-gallon so that you would be relying on actual numbers instead of an assumed number?

Example: The instrument panel on the car near the odometer, which reports the distance traveled, has a button and dial mileage meter you may reset to zero when you fill your gas tank. Then, the next time you fill the tank, write on your receipt the distance driven since the last fill of the gas tank. Your receipt reports to you the number of gallons of fuel you purchased to bring your tank to be full again.

Now, you have the numbers you need to calculate your Miles-per-Gallon.
Let's say the miles on the distance meter read 344 miles.
Next, we divide the number of gallons purchased (15 gallons of fuel) into the number of miles driven, which is 344.

```
    23  Miles Per Gallon
15) 344
    30
     4

    44
    45
```

23 X 15 = 345
This is a proof because multiplication is the other side of division.

We can quickly see that the quotient is rounded up to 23 because the numbers
are so close that we need not say 22.9 Miles-per-Gallon

Now we can multiply this 23 MPG by the 16 gallons in our fuel tank and know
that we can safely drive a certain distance less than probably 340 miles
because you need to always keep enough fuel so you can safely get to
a fuel station.

```
   23
X  16
  138
   23
  368    Expected safe driving distance on a tank of gas
```

So, watch your next fuel tank fills and rework these calculations with
your numbers so you know your expected safe driving distance on a
tank of gas in your car.

Think about what you just learned about how to get the information you
need to use to get to the ultimate answer you need.
Think and then use multiplication and division to get the answer.

~~~~~

We have learned the relationship of multiplication and division.
Each may be seen and understood to be the other side of the first.
One proves the other.

Remember, that this book is intended to provide you with the tools to
develop both math and cognitive thinking skills bordering on excellence,
so that you may improve your problem-solving skills, as this discipline
spreads into other areas of your daily life.

EXERCISE FOUR

4-A Fractions

Proper Fractions

We already talked about fractions. They relate to some amount being part of a whole.

Example: 1/2

This fraction means that we are talking about 1 part of 2.
That could be half of a dollar or 1/2 of one dollar being an amount of $0.50 or as we know to be fifty cents or two quarters.

1/4 means we are talking about 1 part of 4 parts.
That could be a quarter of a dollar or 1/4 of one dollar being an amount.
$.025 or plain .25 meaning one-quarter

These are proper fractions because the top number (numerator) is smaller than the lower number (denominator).

Proper fractions are normal and most common.

We may divide the numerator (top number) by the denominator (bottom number) and the answer will be less than one or a fractional amount.

Example: 1/2   When we divide 1 by 2
Your mind quickly tells you the answer is $0.50 or fifty cents or half a dollar

We arrive at this by dividing:

$$\overline{}$$
2) 1

We quickly see that 2 does not go into 1
So, we fractionalize the 1 by adding a decimal followed by zero

$$\overline{}$$
2) 1.0

When we place a decimal, we also place it directly above the answer line in the same position and we enter the answer to the right of the decimal

So, now we divide 2 into 10 and the answer is 5

```
    .5
_____
2) 1.0
```

The .5 is the same as .50 or as we know to be half a dollar

The .5 is 5 tenths of a dollar also known as 1/2 or 50 cents

The .5 or .50 we also know is 50% (fifty percent) or one-half of dollar

We convert a fraction to a decimal by dividing the lower (larger) number into the (smaller) top number. We saw that above with 1/2.

We can do the same calculation with 1/4
If we wish to convert a fraction to a percent, we continue the above division calculation of dividing 4 into 1.

$$\overline{}$$
4) 1   number 1 is a whole number. There is an invisible decimal after a whole number.

So, to divide, we add the decimal because we know that the answer, we arrive at, has to be and will be less than 1

4 into 1 does not go
So, we add a decimal after the whole number 1
Then, divide 4 into 1.00
Place decimal in answer - above lower decimal
4 into 10 goes 2 with 2 carry down before the zero to the right
4 into 20 = 5
Answer is 0.25

Then we multiply 0.25 by 100 by moving decimal two places to right and adding percent sign to covert the fraction to a decimal and then to a percent.   25%

Remember that Percent means hundred. So, the number before the percent sign is normally less than 100. [There are situations where a percentage is greater than 100% to be addressed later on].

Work this 4 into 1 out on your paper to see how it makes sense

Write out different fractions and divide them and see and understand the constancy of the calculations

----

Over-the-counter-medicines costs vary.
A bottle of 250 vitamins costs $30
Calculate the unit cost of one vitamin.

Divide the number of vitamins into the cost to determine the unit cost.

```
            .1
250 vitamins) $30.00 Cost of the bottle of 250
```

Drop the zero to the right of both numbers

How many 25 are in 30?
1
Place the quotient 1 after the decimal
Subtract 25 from 30
Remainder is 5
Cannot divide 25 into 5
So, bring down a zero
Divide 25 into 50
Answer is 2

Quotient is .12 or $0.12 per vitamin or twelve cents

Proof: 250 vitamins
   X .12   (twelve cents_unit cost of one vitamin)
     $30.00

4-B Improper Fractions

We learned that fractions are proper fractions because the top number (numerator) is smaller than the lower number (denominator).

When we have a fraction with the top number (numerator) larger than the lower number (denominator), it is known as an improper fraction. An improper fraction always equals 1 or more. We know this because it is top-heavy.
When we divide a smaller number into a larger number, the result or answer, known as Quotient, will always equal 1 or more.

8/2 would be an improper fraction

We divide 2 into 8

_4____   Decimal is 4.0
2) 8

2 goes into 8 4 times.

There are 4 2s in 8 (this is simple multiplication) 4 X 2 = 8

When we looked at the times table, we saw this

Numbers are constants.

6/4 would be an improper fraction

We divide 4 into 6 and get 1.5 decimal
Again, this shows that the answer must be more than 1
This answer is 1 [4] and one-half {of the 4} or 1.5
Remember that the .5 is one-half of the number 1

So, we see there are 1 1/2 4s in 6

Proof:

1 X 4 =   4
1/2 of 4 = 2

Total: 6   4 + 2 = 6

We can also just reduce the fraction by the largest common denominator, which is the largest number found in both numbers

6/4   divide each by 2 = 3/2

Divide 2 into 6 = 3 (Note: this is opposite of multiply: 2 X 3 = 6
Divide 2 into 4 = 2   this is opposite of multiply: 2 X 2 = 4)

Divide 2 into 3 and we see 1.5 as decimal (one & one-half) or the same as we know would be $1.50

There are 1 1/2 2s in 3
There is one 2 and there is half of 2 (or 1/2) additional

We know that $1.50 plus $1.50 = $3.00
The two half-dollars = $1 to be added to the 1 [2 X 1/2 = 1] + 2 = $3

The answers in these two examples are the same because the second fraction is half of the first and represents a reduction of both the numerator and the denominator by the same largest common denominator

-----

Mixed Fractions are a combination of a whole number and a partial or fractional number

2 7/8

When we look at this number, we quickly see that it equals just less than three. [8/8 less 7/8 = 1/8
8/8 means 8 of 8 or 100% or all
7/8 means 7 of 8 or a little less than 100% or all
1.8 means 1 of 8 or much less than 100% or all

By 1/8, it is less than 1 to be added to the 2
7/8 + 1/8   Add the top numbers across and you have 8/8, which = 1
We just worked speed math by visualizing what we saw.
When we divide the numerator of 8 by the denominator 8, we see that there is one eight in eight and therefore the answer is number 1.
Divide 8 into 8 = 1 (there is one eight in eight)

Conversion answer by dividing (quotient) is 2.875 as a decimal if you divide it out

Now, we happen to know that 7/8 = 87 1/2 or .875 so, we see the answer
We know this from the Decimal Equivalents Chart we are learning below.

When we look at the fraction 7/8, we can immediately divide 8 into 7 and see that it will not go. So, we divide 8 into 7.0 knowing that the quotient will be less than one because of the decimal. 8 X 9 = 72. This quickly tells us that 9 is too high. Therefore, 8 must be the number with a remainder. So, we enter the 8 and continue dividing the number out. You can work out the rest of this division problem.

87.5 is eighty-seven and one half.

Remember, that .5 is one-half of one (like $0.50 is fifty-cents of $1).

We will see and know this from the Decimal Equivalents Chart we are learning below. (This is repeated for emphasis.)

We have 2 and 7/8

Immediately, I know that 7/8 is 87.5%. Our goal is for you to know this automatically.

What is the decimal equivalent of 7/8? .875 added to the 2 = 2.875

When we divide 8 into 7, we know the answer will be less than 1

    <u>0.875</u>   (.875 is Quotient – result of division)
8)7.000
  <u>64</u>
   60
   <u>56</u>
    40
    <u>40</u>
     0

Calculation: (whole number 2.) + the (7 / 8) = 2.875

We place the fraction in parentheses to show that it is a separate calculation inside the parenthesis.
The calculation is what we see directly above.

When we add mixed fractions:

We must have common denominators (lower number).

Let's say we have fractions:

15 3/4   to add to   16 4/9
Common denominator for 4 and 9 would be 36 (4 times 9)

So, we focus on the inner fraction and restate it with the common denominator so the values remain unchanged.

3/4 and 4/9 fractions become

3/36 + 4/36 = 7/36

We know that the answer will be a decimal and less than 1

We know that 2 X 35 = 70
Since the divisor of 36 is larger than half of 70, we can quickly see that the result or Quotient will be less than 2.

```
      __.194_
  36) 7.000
      3 6
      3 40
      3 24
        160
        144
         16
```

This remainder tells you that 4 goes onward in quotient

6 7/8 = 55/8   (6 X 8 = 48 and add 7 = 55 over 8

```
    _6.875_____
  8)55.000
    48
    70
    64
    60
    56
    40
    40
     0
```

We know from tables that $7/8 = 87.5\%$

When we divide 8 into 55, the answer is greater than 1 because 55/8 is an improper fraction

When we look at the fraction 7/8, we know it means 7 parts of a total of 8. This tells us it is a number with a high percentage, yet still below 1 We will see this more clearly on the Decimal Equivalents chart below.

4-C Decimal Equivalents

Decimal Equivalent of a fraction means it is the other side of a fraction. We practiced this when we divided out a fraction and arrived at a decimal value.

A proper fraction has a numerator (top number) smaller than the denominator (lower number).
As we have learned, when we divide a larger number into a smaller number, we must add a decimal after the smaller number and add zeroes because the answer must be less than one. We also place the decimal directly above in the Quotient.

Then, we divide using long division as we learned above.

3/4 is a fraction we are familiar with. We divide 4 into 3.

```
   .75
4) 3.00      Because 3 is a whole number, place decimal after the 3
   2 8       and directly above and add zeroes to enable division.
    20
    20
     0
```

.75 is the decimal equivalent of fraction ¾. Three out of four total

We instinctively know without thinking this is true,
because we calculate this with quarters of a dollar all the time.

3 $0.25 (twenty-five cent pieces) = $0.75 or seventy-five cents
3/4 of a Dollar, or three-quarters of a Dollar [4 quarters in $1]

Next, is a Decimal Equivalents Chart 4C for you to absorb and learn.

4-D Decimal Equivalents Chart

--

Fraction		Decimal	Fraction		Decimal
1/64	=	0.015625	33/64	=	0.515625
1/32	=	0.03125	17/32	=	0.53125
3/64	=	0.046875	35/64	=	0.546875
1/16	=	0.0625	9/16	=	0.5625
5/64	=	0.078125	37/64	=	0.578125
3/32	=	0.09375	19/32	=	0.59375
7/64	=	0.109375	39/64	=	0.609375
1/8	=	0.125	5/8	=	0.625
9/64	=	0.140625	41/64	=	0.640625
5/32	=	0.15625	21/32	=	0.65625
11/64	=	0.171875	43/64	=	0.671875
3/16	=	0.1875	11/16	=	0.6875
13/64	=	0.203125	45/64	=	0.703125
7/32	=	0.21875	23/32	=	0.71875
15/64	=	0.234375	47/64	=	0.734375
1/4	=	0.25	3/4	=	0.75
17/64	=	0.265625	49/64	=	0.765625
9/32	=	0.28125	25/32	=	0.78125
19/64	=	0.296875	51/64	=	0.796875
5/16	=	0.3125	13/16	=	0.8125
21/64	=	0.328125	53/64	=	0.828125
11/32	=	0.34375	27/32	=	0.84375
23/64	=	0.359375	55/64	=	0.859375
3/8	=	0.375	7/8	=	0.875
25/64	=	0.390625	57/64	=	0.890625
13/32	=	0.40625	29/32	=	0.90625
27/64	=	0.421875	59/64	=	0.921875
7/16	=	0.4375	15/16	=	0.9375
29/64	=	0.453125	61/64	=	0.953125
15/32	=	0.46875	31/32	=	0.96875
31/64	=	0.484375	63/64	=	0.984375
1/2	=	0.5	1	=	1

--

Decimal Equivalents Chart

The most common of the decimal equivalents we use are:

1/8   0.125   See this as 8 X 12 = 96 (of 100) with remainder of 4
And fraction 4/8 we know to reduce by dividing each by a common
number (4) = 1/2 and we know that 1/2 equals .5 or 50%
So, we see that to solve fraction 1/8, we divide 8 into 1.00 and the
answer will always be 0-.125
So, we know that 12 1/2 will always be the equivalent of 1/8

When we look at 1/8 on a ruler, we see it is a small measurement.
A fraction smaller than 1/8 is 1/16. It is half the size of 1/8.
So, when you compare 1/16 to 1/8, we see that the decimal equivalent
is half of the 1/8 decimal equivalent. When you understand this, you
begin to see the relationships in these numbers.

So, we see that in Decimal Equivalents the numbers are the same as
on our measuring instrument or ruler.

The larger the decimal equivalent, the smaller the size.

1/16 is smaller than and therefore half of 1/8
Two X 1/16 = 1/8
1/8 is smaller than and therefore half of 1/4
2 X 1/8 = 1/4
1/4 is smaller than and therefore half of 1/2
2 X 1/4 = 1/2
1/2 is smaller than and therefore half of One whole
2 X 1/2 = 1 whole

So, from the above and when looking at a ruler, we see and know that:

There are 16 1/16 in one inch;
There are   8 1/8 in one inch;
There are   4 1/4 in one inch;
There are   2 1/2 in one inch.

So, we see that 2 1/16 ths fit inside the 1/8 ths & 16 1/16 are inside the
one whole;

The 2 1/8 ths fit inside 1/4 & 8 1/8 are inside the one whole;
The 2 1/4 s fit inside 1/2 & 4 1/4 are inside the one whole;
The 2 1/2 s fit inside the one whole.

We apply this same thought process to each decimal on the Chart.
So, you are encouraged to follow the calculations through on each of
these fractions below to master this way of thought.

So, let's build up the scale of sizes:

1/16 1/16 is very small 0.0625
1/8 This is twice 1/16   1/16 + 1/16 = 2/16 then reduced = 1/8 12.5%
1/4 This is twice 1/8   1/8 + 1/8 = 2/8 then reduced = 1/4   25%
1/2 This is twice 1/4   1/4 + 1/4 = 2/4 then reduced = 1/2   50%
1   This is twice 1/2   1/2 + 1/2 = 2/2 then reduced = 1   100%

3/8   This is three X 1/8
So, if 1/8 = 12.5 or 12 1/2, then 3 X 12.5 = (3 x 12 = 36 and 3 X .5 = 1.5
So, we add 36 plus 1.5 = 37.5 or 37.5%

Recall, that numbers are constant in their relationship to each other.

Work this out on your paper.

Think about what the fraction tells you. Are you close to number one or
100%? How close?

Work out the same calculation using fractions below.

Challenge yourself to think and work this out on these:

7/16 This is less, though very close to half, which would be 8/16

9/16 This fraction signals more than half, which would be 8/16 or 1/2

5/8 This fraction signals more than half, which would be 4/8 or 1/2

3/4 This signals more than half, which would be 2/4 or reduced ½

7/8 This fraction is again very close to 8/8 so, percent is high 87.5%

1/7 This fraction is much less than half, so its percentage is 14.3%
and will be on the low side of the range of 7 as 1 of 7 or the 14.3%
It would be the other side of 6/7 85.7%
14.3 + 85.7 = 100 or 100%

When you learn and become versed in these most common of the
decimal equivalents,
you will better understand fractions, decimals and percentages. Study
and learn these so you recognize them for what they tell you at first
glance. They help you estimate on the spot.

Here is an application of what we have learned.
The circle walking path in the park is 1/8 of a mile.
** Remember, that the larger the denominator (lower number in a
fraction),
the smaller is the size or dimension or distance. 1/8 means one of 8
pieces of pie.
for example. 1/4 means one of four pieces of pie. 1/2 means 1 of 2
pieces of pie**

Calculate the number of times we must walk around the circle path to
reach one mile.

Averages, Estimates, Rounding

4-E Averaging
Add a series of numbers and divide by the number of numbers in the list to calculate the average.

An airplane and a hiking problem were discussed earlier. The airplane situation laid out the formula for you to calculate average weight.

Add first and then divide by the number of entries to calculate average.

73
27
64
51
<u>33</u>   add the column
    Total

Divide the Total by the number of entries to arrive at Average.

A bundle of bananas holds 14 bananas
The bundle is sold by the pound at a rate of $0.70 per pound
The bundle weighs 2 pounds
Calculate the total cost of a bundle of bananas purchase:
Calculate the average cost of one banana:

When you look at a pattern in a list of averaging, you may see how easily you may estimate and find yourself close to a number.

When we average, we seek a middle number in a series or pattern. So, without calculating, look for the mid-range number and estimate.

4-F Estimating

When we estimate in our minds, we seek to arrive at a number close to the actual number. That is what is an estimate.

73
64
51
33
27

Estimate the average in this column above

Then, refer to your previous calculation of Average to see how close you may be to the actual average number.

Sometimes when we estimate, we round up or down. What that means is that if a decimal amount is below .50 or 50% [one-half], then we round down to the nearest whole number. If a decimal amount is above .50 or 50%, then we round up the answer to the nearest whole number.

4-G Rounding
If we see a number to be $9.87, we may round up and say it is near $10 or about $10 or just under $10. Or $10. That would be rounding up.

If we see a number to be $8.16, we may round down and say it is near $8 or about $8 or just over $8. That would be rounding down.

Rounding helps you when you are doing a quick calculation and want to evaluate a price or an opportunity by calculating a relative figure and not the exact number for your answer. It speeds up your thought process leading to an answer.

4-H Ratios

A ratio compares two differences in a relationship. It shows the number of times one number may be in another.

Example
You may purchase three boxes of cereal and one gallon of milk.

The cereal cost: 3 for $15.32

The milk cost: 1 for $2.87

Product ratio is written as a comparison as 3:1 or 1:3

Ratio tells us there are three cereals for every 1 milk.

Cost ratio is written as a comparison as $2.87: $15.32
or $15.32: $2.87

We can reduce down to determine the unit cost of 1 cereal.
Visualize the rounded ratio of 3:15 and that there are three in the 15.
3 cereals for $15 would be $5 per cereal.
So, visualize the ratio as 3:5 with equal quantities.
Then, see that 5 divided by 3 tells you that the cost of one cereal is just more than 1 1/2 the cost of one milk.

Ratio tells us the cereal cost is approximately: Milk $3 rounded X 150% the cost of milk equals $1.50 more than the $3 cost of the milk to approximate the cost of one cereal. $3 + $1.50 = $4.50

This is the first time we see a percentage greater than 100%.
We just calculated that the $4.50 is 150% of $3.00
Think about this.

Long Division:

```
     ___._____
2.87) 15.32
```

First: move decimal in divisor (2.87) two digits to right
Second: move decimal in dividend (15.32) two digits to right

```
     _____._____
287) 1532.
```

Third: place decimal above for the answer (quotient)
Fourth: divide 1532 by 287

Here is where I estimate the answer in advance.
287 is close to 300
So, if I were to round up the 287 to 300 and divide,
my quick estimate would be the answer would be 5 with a fractional
amount over five because 300 X 5 = 1500 and we are at 1532

Fourth: So, we enter 5 above the 2 and before the decimal in the
quotient,
and multiply the five X 287 and then subtract 1435 from 1532 to learn
the
remaining fractional amount over five, which is 97

```
     ___ 5._____
287) 1532.
  -   1435
        97
```

Fifth: We are unable to divide 287 into 97
Therefore, we bring down a zero after the 97

```
     ___ 5._____
287) 1532.0
```

```
-   1435
      97 0
```

Sixth: divide 970 by 287 and
My estimate similar to the previous would see the answer as 3 because
300 (287 rounded up) in 1970 would be (300 X 3 = 900)
So, I enter 3 above the fractional zero and multiply

This is what we call long division

```
        ___ 5.3_____
287) 1532.0
   -   1435
         97 0
   -     861
          109 remainder
```

Seventh: We look at the remainder of 109 and estimate that it is closer
to the 287 than the previous remainders. Thus, we may estimate that
the next calculation would be the same as the 3 we just entered.
Therefore, we may choose to not add another zero after the 1532.0 and
bring the zero down making the remainder 2480 and divide again
unless we definitely need to know the next number in the Quotient.
If we were to estimate again based on our rounded up 287 being 300,
we would conclude that the next digit in the quotient would be 3.
This is because our rounded-up 300 divisor for estimating purposes
would be divided into 109 for answer (quotient) of 3.

```
        ___ 5.33_____   Quotient
287) 1652.00           Dividend; 2897 is Divisor
   -   1435
         97 0
   -     86 1
          109 remainder
```

There may be 24 students to 1 teacher is classroom
The ratio is 24:1   or 1:24

For 1 teacher there are 24 students

The large school bus holds 48 adults (2 to a seat)

The large school bus holds 72 children (3 per seat)

The ratios are: 1 bus driver for 48 adults   1:48

                          1 bus driver for 72 children   1:72

A bundle of bananas holds 14 bananas
Seven students will share the 14 bananas

The ratio is: 7:14 or 14:7
The ratio may be reduced because each number is divisible by 7

14:7 = 2:1

We wish to use the lowest common denominator numbers in ratio

Conclusion: Ratio tells us there are 2 bananas for every 1 student.

A poll was conducted on a sidewalk to gather information about how members of the general public feel about a certain matter or question. One question was asked, seeking a quick answer. The quick answer did not allow time for thoughtful consideration in the belief that the response may be more-true for the respondent.

56 Answers were affirmative
10 Answers were negative
14 Answers were ambiguous – or, no opinion
80 Persons were questioned

So, the ratio of 56:10 tells us that:
56 persons of 80 persons were affirmative
with ten persons of 80 being negative
and 14 persons unsure

We can reduce an Improper fraction of 56/10
Move the decimal one place to the left in the 10
And move decimal one place to the left in the 56
That tells us that the ratio is 5.6 persons answered affirmative
for one person negative

Calculate the percentage of 80 persons represented in the:
Number of 56 affirmative
Number of 01negative
Number of 14 unsure

.7   .0125.175   Prove your answers

~~~~~~~~~~~~~

4-I Reciprocal

Reciprocal of a number always = 1

1/2 and 2/1 multiplied out is 2/2 = 1

The reciprocal of any fraction is to reverse the position of the numbers.
The numerator becomes the denominator and vice versa.
Then each cancels the other out crosswise
Or we multiply the two numerators and multiply the two denominators
And the answers are equal with one above the other
A fraction composed of two identical numbers equals 1
1/1 = 1
2/2 = 1
8/8 = 1
32/32 = 1

Reciprocals in business are the other side of an agreement or position intended to be nearly or exactly equal. Reciprocity exists when mutual benefits to all parties are the foundation of an agreement.

4-J Percentages

A percentage is a number representing a portion of a larger number, normally 100.
A percentage may be larger than 100%
It is like saying 40/100 (40 of 100) is 40%
That means that 4 out of every ten or 40 out of every hundred.
A percentage is another way of expressing a fraction or decimal.

We calculate a percentage by dividing the 100% number or denominator into the smaller number. It is the number below the angle line in a fraction.

Percentages speak to probability or part of an actual number or amount.

The Weather Report provides a probability of a change in the weather. For example,
the storm may arrive at a certain time based on the speed of its movement across the country – a 30% probability so, the odds are 3 out of ten that the storm will arrive;
there is a 70% probability of rain changing to sleet and then to snow so, the odds are 7 out of 10 it will storm;
there is an 80% probability that cloud cover may prevent persons in a certain geographical area from seeing a meteor or the International Space Station so, the odds are 8 out of 10 that the cloud cover will be thick;
or other reports.

Sports betting pays winnings based on the odds of a team winning. The odds are based on actual performance or a supported belief, or an unsupported belief (termed a hunch) that a certain outcome will be witnessed. The odds represent a percentage of probability as to outcome of a certain event.

People gamble and bet against the odds because they seek the larger payoff, if they beat the odds.

On the weather report, we see a percentage of probability of rain, snow, violent storm, heat wave and otherwise.

In our vehicles, we see a percentage of power in the car battery, and fuel in the gas tank.

In business, we are given performance probabilities when we receive bids on a construction job. The many variables are the basis of unsure conditions that may delay completion. A Gannt chart offered with the bid may present a number of if-come probability scenarios because of the unknowns that may arise and require modification of the initial plan.

In geographic areas where the winter season may be brutal, plans for construction and completion of a building may project 50% of heavy cement construction to be completed before inclement weather so that the building may be enclosed for inside work during winter months.

You check your smart phone to know the percentage of battery life remaining so that you do not run out of power.

ODDS
The odds are low that a gambler will win in a casino.
Yet, we do know that some gamblers do win in a casino.
Therefore, people go to gamble in a casino with the expectation that they will lose because the odds are stacked in favor of the casino and therefore the casino wins nearly all the time.
The casino has to let some gamblers win or nobody would gamble.
So, the history of probabilities suggests that someone will win in the casino today. The amount of the win and the time is unknown.
This probability calls to gamblers to go to the casino in the hopes that they will be the persons there when the probability of win becomes real and they win and the casino loses.
These people play the percentages and hope to win and generally do not expect to win in the casino.

CONVERT TO PERCENTAGE

100% of anything (objects or persons or places) is the total.
5/20 means 5 out of 20

Divide:
```
       _ .25__  or 25% or what we know to be 1/4
   20) 5.00
       4 0
       100
       100
         0
```

5 is whole number not divisible by 20.
So, add decimal to indicate less than 1 and add zero(es).

We see that 5 is 1/4 of 20 because 5 X 4 = 20

We convert a decimal to a percentage by moving the decimal two places to the right and adding the percent sign %.

We convert a percentage to a decimal by removal of the percent sign and moving the decimal two places to the left.

We convert fractions to decimal before to a percentage.
A percentage is another way of stating a decimal amount.

Think about percentages as a portion of a whole and see a fraction or a percentage that way for they are basically the same because one is the conversion of the other. Know the common Decimal Equivalents we reviewed on the earlier chart.

Common Decimals   Percentages   Fractions

.05	5%	5/100 reduced to 1/20
.10	10%	10/100 reduced to 1/10
.20	30%	20/100 reduced to 1/5
.25	25%	25/100 reduced to 1/4
.50	50%	50/100 reduced to 1/2
.75	75%	75/100 reduced to 3/4

We convert mixed fractions to percent.
In a mixed fraction, the whole number is the quotient.
The numerator (top number in the fraction) is remainder
The denominator (lower number in the fraction)

Multiply whole number Quotient by Denominator
And add the numerator
That creates fraction of the result / over denominator
Divide the fraction by 100

16 2/3% = (16 x 3) = 48
Add numerator   2
             50

Divide the result by denominator

    16.66
3) 50.

Divide by 100 by moving decimal 2 spaces to left

So, we see that 16 x 6 = 96
.66 X 6 = 3.96 or rounded to be 4 -6+4 = 100

Therefore 16 2/3 = fraction of 1/6 as we see on Decimal Equivalent Chart

We refer to this same formula to convert any improper fraction.

Earlier, in ratios we discussed that a percentage may be greater than 100%.

We learned that an improper fraction exists when the numerator (top number) is greater than the denominator (lower number).

When we divide an improper fraction, we know that the number will be greater than 1 or 100%.

Example: 5/3

We immediately know that three divides into 5 with quotient of 1 to begin with and that there will be a remainder. When we divide 5 by 3, the 1 tells us that the quotient will be more than 1. This is saying the same thing twice for emphasis.

$$3 \overline{)5}$$

We know we must place decimal after the five and above in the quotient because the divisor (3) is less than the dividend (5) and we know that there will be a remainder to extend the long division problem

$$3 \overline{)5.0}$$

```
   1.
3)5.0
   3
   2 remainder
```

```
   1.
3)5.0
   3
   2 0 bring down the zero to divide for fractional amount over 100
```

```
   1.6
3)5.0
   3
   2 0
   18
   2 Remainder tells us that the calculation continues as 6666
```

So, we know that the Quotient is 1.66

When we move decimal 2 places to right (2 places = hundreds), then we add the percent sign and see that the percent is 166%.

This calculation tells us that 5 is 166% greater than 3.

Proof: 3 X 1.66 = 4.98   4.98 rounded up is the while number 5

A product normally sells for $4. It is on clearance sale for $1.
Calculate the percentage of discount,

4 − 1 = 3
So, the discount is $3 of the $4 normal price

3/4 would be the fraction
You should instinctively know that the proper fraction 3/4 is 75%
Just as $0.75 is seventy-five cents or 3/4 of a dollar.
The other side of the transaction is the $1 of $4 to be your cost.
The fraction 1/4 is one of 4 or 25% or $0.25 or same as one quarter of a dollar

So, if you paid 25% for the product, your discount was 75%.
Also, if your discount was 75%, your cost was 25%
Numbers always add up.
25% plus 75% = 100%

What is the percentage of your purchase price that you saved?
$3 saved / divided by $1 paid creates an improper fraction.
We discussed that an improper fraction always equals more than 100%
1 divided into 3 = 3.00 and when we move the decimal two spaces to the right for a percentage, we know it is 300%

Earlier, we talked about the unusual conditions under which a percentage may be greater than 100% and here is an example.

We know that $6.30 is the amount to pay after taking a 30% Discount.
Yet, we do not know the normal selling price of the item.
Calculate the normal selling price of the item.

$6.30 is after 30% Discount off of an unknown selling price.
The other side of 30% is 70%
70% is the amount of the $6.30 because we know that 30% represents the amount of the discount
So, we divide 6.30 by 70%

70% becomes .70) 6.30
Move .70 decimal two places to the right
Move 6.30 decimal two places to the right
We then have:

```
 _____
70)630.
```

```
   ___9.___
70)630.
   630
```

This calculation tells us that $9 is the normal price

Proof:
9 x 70% = 6.30   Actual cost after Discount applied
9 X 30% = 2.70   The Discount Amount
Add the two and see they equal $9.00

4-K Measure

When we look at a tape measure or a ruler, it is about measurement.
We must learn how to read a tape measure. The measure is a
fractional part of a whole of something. It shows you fractions in a
straight line.

A tape measure may be of fabric used in the garment industry; folding
and expandable hinged wood used in construction; roll up metal ruler
used in construction; a wooden ruler used in school or home and
sometimes called a straight-edge; a corner-square or other various-
sized metal or plastic pieces; or consistent marks on something.
Each tape measure or ruler measures in standard and commonly-used
one-inch increments. One side of the ruler may measure in millimeters.
2 ½ millimeters approximate one inch. So, obviously, millimeters are

more precise than inches. Millimeters are used when making fine machine-tolerance measurements.

Let's look at one inch.
One inch has lines representing:
1/2 inch   Two half-inches = 1 inch
1/4 inch   Four quarter-inch = 1 inch
             Two quarter-inch = 1/2 inch

1/8 inch   Eight one-eighth inches = 1 inch
             Four one-eighth inches = 1/2 inch
             Two one-eighth inches = 1/4 inch

1/16 inch   Sixteen one-sixteenth inches = 1 inch
             Eight one-sixteenth inches = 1/2 inch
             Four one-sixteenth inches = 1/4 inch
             Two one-sixteenth inches = 1/8 inch

When we look at these numbers and think about what we see, the higher the denominator (lower number) the smaller the increment. So, 1/16 is smaller than 1/8, which is smaller than 1/4, which is smaller than 1/2, which is smaller than 1 whole. This is why we see that there are two 1/16 in 1/8 and two 1/8 in 1/4 and two 1/4 in 1/2 and two 1/2 in 1. Think through this and see the relationships and constancy.

The roll up metal ruler used in construction is marked at 16-inch increments because this is the standard measurement between the center of wall studs.

Study a ruler and understand these dimensions.
Use a ruler to measure the size of a standard letter size page.
It will read 8 1/2 inches wide by 11 inches long.
Some legal documents are 8 1/2 inches wide by 14 inches long.
It will be beneficial for you to know and understand how to use a ruler or tape measure. Understanding this will help you to be able to judge

space or distance quickly, without relying on a ruler to measure. When you do this, you would be estimating or approximating.

In our daily lives, we visualize and actually measure or we estimate measurements of all sorts of items, spaces, places and more.

Take a tape measure and measure the furniture in your home.
Measure the length, width, height and see the space they take up in a room.
Measure the distance between the walls to see the size of the room.
Measure the width of the sidewalk cement squares.
Measure the doors in your home and see if they are all the same size or different sizes and figure out why some may be wider.
Measure family members height to see how tall they are.
Measure the length, width and height of a large vehicle to see whether it would fit into the garage before trying to get it inside.

Distance is generally measured in miles.
One mile is 5,280 feet
A town or city may be reported as having the size of square miles.
A square mile is a unit of measure applied to real estate meaning that it would be a square with each of the four sides being one mile.

The moon is about 239,000 miles from earth
The sun is about 93 million miles from earth (93,000,000)
The circumference of the earth is about 25,000 miles.
Travelers plan trips according to the distance to the destination and also to various places once they reach their destination.

Look at a paper map and see distances between places and cities.
See the highways stretching the distance of the countryside.

Larger measurements than inches and distances are measured in feet. So, we must look at and see the inches in one foot.

6 inches equals one-half (1/2) of one foot. 6 inches of 12 inches, which is one foot.
12 inches equals 1 foot in length
Now we can multiply or add as the numbers rise.
18 inches equals 1 1/2 feet.
 24 inches equals 2 feet
The numbers continue to rise as the number of feet (or fractional number of feet) increase
72 inches is 6 feet in length
Inches and feet are shown on long rulers.

We measure to determine the amount of building materials needed for construction.
We measure the cost of a project against our financial resources to determine whether to begin construction.

4-L Time Management

Each person has 24 hours a day.
Clocks are either 24-hour or 12-hour.
We refer to AM and PM on a 12-hour clock.
AM is abbreviation for Ante Meridian or before midday.

Midday is when the sun passes from east to west across the Prime Meridian.
The Prime Meridian is a certain point on a vertical line running from the North Pole to the South Pole.
It passes through Greenwich, England and also Accra, Ghana in Africa.
I stood at the Prime Meridian site in Accra, Ghana in early September, 2011.
The Prime Meridian separates the earth portions into Eastern and Western Hemispheres.

PM is abbreviation for Post Meridian or after meridian.
So, PM means after 12:00 or Noon or midday
This is true on a 12 or 24-hour clock.
We just do not have to say PM when referring to the time on a 24-hour clock because 12:00 or Noon or midday is followed by 1:00 PM on a 12-hour clock and followed by 13:00 hours on a 24-hour clock.

Military uses 24-hour clocks for certainty and to remove question as to whether time is AM or PM. 24-hour time begins at midnight known as 0 hours and ends at 24 hours the next night at midnight.
So, we learn that 11:40 AM on a 12-hour clock is 11:40 on a 24-hour clock. 2:40 PM on a 12-hour clock we normally use would be 14:40 on a 24-hour clock. (12 Noon + 2 hours 40 minutes)

Thus, 4:43 PM on a 12-hour clock would be 16:43 hours on a 24-hour clock. Determined by 12 Noon = 12 hours + 4 hours (1-4) = 16 hours and then we enter the minutes of 43 to read 16:43 hours

We left for a drive at 10:14 hours and arrived at 16:02 hours.
Calculate drive time: hours   minutes   Show your calculations.

5:48

Exam began at 08:07 hours and ended at 13:02 hours
Break times during the exam totaled 36 minutes
Calculate exam time in room: 4 hours: 55 minutes = 100%
Calculate percentage of time at tables: 4 hours 19 minutes
4.55 - .36 = 4.19
4.19/4.55 = 92%

Calculate percentage of break time to time in room:

36/4.55   //   7.9%

92% + 7.9% = 99.9%

5 hours (- .07 + .02 = -.05) or 4:55 minutes

~~~~~

You have 24 hours each day.
The purpose of discussing time management is to alert you to its importance in your life. Look at the number of hours daily that you devote to people and activities that benefit or will benefit you. That is a good focus.   You may need to think about whether other people or activities are distractions, which fail to move you closer to your personal goals. Each of us needs to place distractions as a low priority in our lives. To do this, it is up to you to define your distractions, which may be consuming your waking hours (and possibly your sleep time) while possibly clouding your mind from what is or has been important to you.

4-M Calendar

Calendar Months:

1	January	31 Days
2	February	28 Days and in Leap Year 29
3	March	31 Days
4	April	30 Days
5	May	31 Days
6	June	30 Days
7	July	31 Days
8	August	31 Days
9	September	30 Days
10	October	31 Days
11	November	30 Days
12	December	31 Days

Twelve Months in the year
Total Days in Year 365

Thirty Days has September, April, June and November; all the rest have Thirty-one Days except February that has 28 and in Leap-Year 29.
Learn this statement and you will always know the number of days in each month.

First Quarter of the Year: Months Numbers 1, 2 and 3
Second Quarter of the Year: Months Numbers 4, 5 and 6
Third Quarter of the Year is: Months Numbers: you enter:
Fourth Quarter of the Year is: Months Numbers: you enter:

March 31 is one-quarter-way through the year.
June 30 is half-way through the year.
September 30 is three-quarters through the year.
December 31 is the 365-th day in the year.

Learn which digit represents each of the twelve months of the year.
Practice, state and know which quarter each month is in.

See, think and understand how the months days repeat as they begin through the week.
You can be creative and make a Universal Calendar because months' days repeat.

4-N WEATHER MAP INTERPRETATION

We are privileged to enjoy detailed weather and forecasts by meteorologists. It is important that you devote yourself to study the maps to learn what they tell you. When you do this, you may someday save your life or the lives of others.

Below is a Weather Report provided by MSN to the general public on the Internet.

--

Today	Mon 24	Tue 25	Wed 26	Thu 27
77° 54°	78° 55°	77° 57°	64° 44°	54° 43°

Moderate >
Sunny
0%

Summary   Hourly   More details

	7:53 AM			73°	76°	75°	6:41 PM			Today	Mon 24	

55° 56° 64° 73° 76° 75° 69° 64° 60° 58° 56° 55°

Now	9 AM	11 AM	1 PM	3 PM	5 PM	7 PM	9 PM	11 PM	1 AM	3 AM	5 AM
–	0%	0%	0%	0%	0%	0%	0%	0%	0%	0%	0%

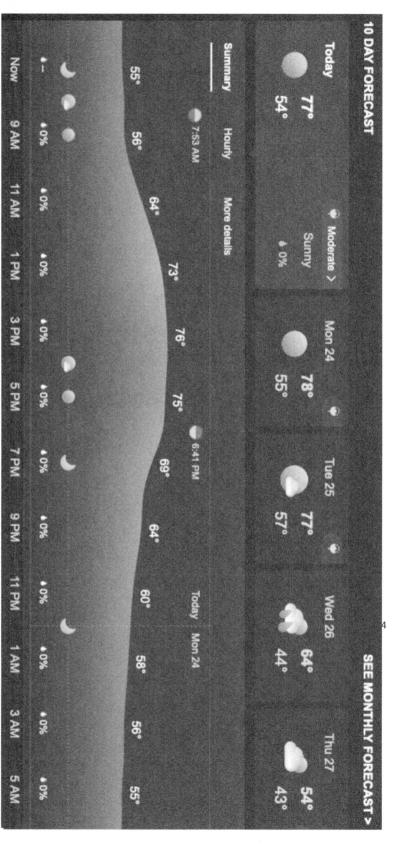

--

This weather map is part of a 10-day forecast. It shows the present and expected weather pattern for a series of days: Sunday, today; Monday; Tuesday; Wednesday; and Thursday.

The report tells us:
Sunrise at 7:53 AM and Sunset at 6:41 PM
These times quickly tell us that the 12-hour daylight days of summer are gone for now as we are into the Fall Season of the year 2022.
Temperature range of each day so we can plan our days and what to wear and where to go and how to get there.
No precipitation today and none expected until Wednesday.
The daily high temperature for today through Tuesday will be at least 77 degrees Fahrenheit.
The daily low temperature for today through Tuesday is expected to be in the range of 54 to 57 degrees through Tuesday.
A cold front is approaching and it will drop the daily temperature down for Wednesday to 64 degrees and a cold 44 degrees Wednesday night.
The cold front will probably stall over the reporting area and drop the Thursday temperatures to a day of 54 degrees and 43 Thursday night.

This information tells us that we have three very pleasant mid-to-high 70s days before two ten-degree lesser days coming up on Wednesday and Thursday for us to plan for as cooler days and nights.

The lower part of the screen pictures a graphic rise in the Sunday daily temperature as the day heats up from 55 degrees to the forecast 77 degrees around 3 to 4 PM.

Let's calculate the temperature range and see what it tells us.

Sunday through Tuesday we can take the average for night and day...
Night: 54 + 55 + 57 = 166   166 divided by 3 = 55 degrees average
Day: 77 + 78 + 77 = 232   232 divided by 3 = 77 We knew it!

77 -55 = 22 degrees daily range

22 divided by 55 = 40% The percentage of 55 the temperature rose on each of the three warmest days
We prove the 40% by:

```
  55              55
X 40%        is .40
              22.00
```

Multiplication proves division

Temp dropped from 77 Tuesday to 64 degrees Wednesday
Calculate the percentage of the drop

77 – 64 = 13 degrees
Divide: the base number 77 into 13

```
        16
77)13.00        We add the zeroes after the decimal because we know
    77                The quotient will be less than one
    53          remainder; So, we bring down the other zero

    530         We know 6 X 8 + 48 So, let's enter 6 in quotient
    462
     68 remainder
```

So, we can say that the13 degree drop is about 16 to 17% of the former 77-degree day temperature

```
Proof:  77 X 16%  is    77
                     X .16
                      462
                       77
                     1232
```

Now we bring down the decimal of the.16 and enter it and find that 16% of 77 degrees is more than 12 degrees and approximately the 13

You may wish to work these same formulas across all the days and learn by taking the initiative to do so now.

You may note that above the hourly entries is 0% probability of precipitation through 5 AM Monday.

Let's take a moment and think of what this would tell us if the numbers were different.
Probability of precipitation tells us:
0% = no precipitation
10 to 15% = very low possibility
25% = low possibility as odds would be 1 out of 4 possibilities
50% = probably as odds would be 1 out of 2 possibilities
75% = high probability as odds would be more than 7 out of 10 possibilities
90% = expect rain now
100% = Rain is falling right now

The other elements of the weather not presented on this screen include Wind direction and velocity,
Air quality, Humidity, Visibility, Humidity, Barometric Pressure. Each of these are worthy of your study.

EXERCISE FIVE

Common Calculation Challenges

These are thinking problems intended to stimulate your mind and strengthen your mental acuity.
They are here as an exam for you to complete and review and even redo to assure yourself that you understand.

Lift each of these problems onto your own page and thoughtfully work it through.

Because answers may be a crutch, refer to them after your work. Ask someone to review your math calculations for assurance of your understanding and so that you reap the rewards of your studies.

Think clearly about the lesson and message in each scenario.

Remember, this book is intended to provide you with the tools to develop math and thinking skills bordering on excellence and with problem solving skills. To become the expert you choose to be, you must think and work through each problem to benefit yourself.

The discipline of *simple math* may spill over into your habits and patterns of behavior in your personal life.

5-A

 Ford, General Motors and Chrysler Production/Sales Statistics:

Ford:

2021 1,905,955 vehicles A
2020 1,700,000 vehicles D

General Motors:

2021 2,218,000 vehicles B
2020 6,800,000 vehicles E

Chrysler:

2021 1,767,396 vehicles C
2020 1,820,443 vehicles F

Lift the production stats by year and add.
Manually calculate Total Production/Sales for each year:

2021   5,891,351 Add A B C
2020 10,320,443 Add D E F
Total   Two Years

Prove your numbers:

16,211,794

Using above production numbers, manually calculate Market-share Percentage, Rounded
We do this by adding each year and then dividing the total into the total for each company
We do this by dividing the larger number into the smaller number because we know that the Quotient must be less than 1

Ford:

2021 32%   Example: 5891351 1905955 =
2020

General Motors:

2021
2020

Chrysler:

2021
2020

Manually calculate Market-share Percentage of Change
Calculate the difference amount between the two years
Divide the difference by the first year to determine percentage

Be alert that the market difference may be a plus or a minus and that determines the character of the Percentage of Change
Thus, some answers may be a % increase and some a % decrease

 Example: Ford: Difference between A & D
 Divide the difference by earlier year (D)

Ford:

2021 12% increase 2021 over 2020   Prove your percentage.

2020

General Motors:

2021
2020

Chrysler:

2021
2020

Manually calculate corporate percentage of 2-years' total production

Ford

General Motors

Chrysler

Prove your calculation.

Think about and interpret what these statistics tell you about these three companies and their production/sales trends.

5-B

We have a grass-roots project to create and build.

Plan   42 hours
Purchases 11 hours
Assemble   96 hours
Paint   27 hours

Calculate the Total Hours
Calculate the percentages of the Total Hours for each line

Enter your calculated percentage of the whole:

Plan
Purchases
Assemble
Paint

Prove your calculation.

5-C

Seven of us went ice-fishing for 4 hours.
The ice was 9-inches thick.

A caught 11 fish
B caught 3 fish
C caught 17 fish
D caught 22 fish
E moved around and caught 67 fish
F caught 9 fish
G caught 34 fish

Calculate the total fish caught: +
Calculate the average number of fish each caught:
   Divide Number Fish by Number of...____

Calculate the percentage of fish each person caught:
  Divide each catch by T...____

Calculate the average number of fish caught per hour:
  Divide Number Fish by Number of ...____

Please Round your answers, if appropriate.

5-D

We went boating upstream from Detroit to Port Huron, MI.
The distance is 64 miles one way.
The downbound water current speed is 10 MPH.
We motored upstream for 6 hours.
We motored downstream for 5 hours.

Round up or down

Distance = Rate X Time
Rate = Distance / Time
Time = Distance / Rate

D	R	T
64	11	6
64	13	5

How do you calculate the speed?

Think about what this tells you about what effect, if any, the current had to do with time, speed, and fuel consumption boating up and down the route?

Did we travel faster going upstream or downstream? Why?

5-E

We took a drive along the lake.
The fog was dense and reduced our visibility and our speed.
Normally it takes us 3 hours to drive the 130 miles.
Due to fog, we arrived in 5 hours.
Calculate our speed.
Distance = Rate X Time

D   R   T
130

             26

             43

Prepare fraction and calculate the percentage of additional time
we drove due to fog: Prove your answer.

2 h/3 h

   _.6_____
3)2.0
    18
     2

So, we know this division will continue as .6666 or rounded to .67 or
67%

Proof:

 .67
X 3
201 or rounded down to whole number 2
and, 2 hours is the number, of additional time driven over three hours

Kroger and many companies earn 2% on their sales – not very much for a year in business. However, if the numbers are large enough, then it suddenly certainly becomes worth the effort.
Yet, they need to market and advertise to retain customers and attract new customers to assure high gross sales of goods and earn the 2%.

Kroger Year 2021 Fourth-Quarter Sales: $33.0 billion A
Kroger Year 2020 Fourth-Quarter Sales: $30.7 billion B
Kroger Year 2019 Fourth-Quarter Sales: $28.9 billion C

Calculate Dollar Increase in Sales:

One Year: 2019
            2020
Difference
Difference divided by earlier of the 2 years
Percentage of Increase or Decrease: Example: 6% increase
    Proof: 28.9 X 6% = 1.7 billion increase (rounded)
               30.7 – 28.9 = 1.8 (fractional difference of .10 or less)

One Year: 2020
            2021
Difference
Difference divided by earlier of the 2 years
Percentage of Increase or Decrease:

Two Year: 2019
            2021
Difference
Difference divided by earlier of the 3 years
Percentage of Increase or Decrease:

Prepare a fraction and calculate the percentage of increase:
Fraction shows plan to divide difference by Total.
Do these statistics reveal a favorable or unfavorable performance?

Think about companies you know about and check to see their financial performance and profitability. Companies close when they are not profitable.

5-G

Work time required before a personal day off is 3 months
How close are you getting to a day off after working 5 weeks?
Calculate remaining weeks to work:
Prepare fraction and calculate percentage of personal day earned:
Prepare fraction and calculate percentage of personal day unearned:

Prove your answer.

$3 \times 4 = 12$
5/12

```
      .4           Quotient is .4 or 40% approximately earned
12)5.0
    48
     2   this remainder is small-to-negligible right now
```

100% less 40% = 60% of days off unearned

5-H

State the number of hours in a day:

State the number of days in a year:

Calculate the number of hours in a week:

Calculate the number of hours in a 30-day month:

Calculate the number of hours in each Quarter of the year
using a standard 30-day month:

Calculate the number of hours in one-half a year
using a standard 30-day month:

Calculate the number of hours in a year:

Calculate the number of waking hours in a year if a person
Sleeps 8-hours nightly:

Prove your calculations.

5-I

Hours on social media during an average day total 9 hours.
Calculate and round your answer for the percentage of a day
on social media:

Think of all you could learn or accomplish in those 9 hours.

Calculate the Total number of hours in a year:

Calculate the total number of hours a person would spend on
Social media in a year at 9-hours per day:

Calculate the percentage of Total annual hours available that a person
would spend on social media in a year at 9 hours per day:

5-J

Food product label states 200 calories in two teaspoons.
Calculate the number of calories consumed in one-half teaspoon.

Prove your answer.

5-K

What hour of the day is Noon during your day?
When does evening start?
How many hours are normally between Noon and Evening?

5-L

Seven 18-wheel 53-foot-long semi-trailers left Pittsburgh for Omaha.
Each trailer weighs approximately 5 tons not loaded.
Each trailer may carry 16 tons of cargo.
The Distance is 915 miles on I-80.
I-80 is a Toll Road west from Youngstown, Ohio about 240 miles on the
Ohio Turnpike to where it meets the Indiana Toll Road and continues
onward into Nebraska where the speed limit rises from 70 MPH to 75
MPH. Drivers continued at 70 MPH the entire route.
Estimated time for driving straight through is 14 hours.
All trailers departed Pittsburgh at the same time in a caravan.
All trailers arrived in Omaha at the same time 19 hours later.
Distance = Rate X Time

State the average speed across the distance of the route.

Cargo is:
Trailer 1   4,000 pounds – small stamping machine
Trailer 2   8,000 pounds – 2 vehicles
Trailer 3   10,000 pounds – 1 open flatbed
Trailer 4   9,000 pounds – 3 boats
Trailer 5   7 tons of brass
Trailer 6   10 tons of copper plate
Trailer 7   16 tons of copper tubing

State the number of pounds in one ton:

Convert pounds to tons
Convert tons to pounds

Calculate Average of all the trailer cargo weights-
In pounds: In tons:
Please Round numbers

Calculate the percentage of each trailer to the whole
In pounds: In tons:
Please Round Percentages up or down

Calculate the total number of tires on all the trailers

Calculate the percent of the total tires on each trailer

Hint: remember we looked at decimal equivalents and
How to convert them to a percent.

Prove your Answers

	Pounds	Tons
Trailer 1	4,000	
Trailer 2		
Trailer 3		
Trailer 4		
Trailer 5		
Trailer 6		
Trailer 7		

Total:

Average is Total divided by ....

Percentage (rounded) is each divided by Total ...

Total Tires:

Percentage (rounded) Tires is each divided by Total ...
  Could it be 14%? If so, for which trailer?

5-M

Event Tickets are $65
Immediate payment discount is 9%
Calculate Amount of Discount:
Calculate net amount due for tickets:

Prove your answer

5-N

How many letters in the Alphabet?
Write the letters

5-O

3 X 16 = 48 (3 X 6=18, post the 8 and carry the one
            3 X 1=3 + the 1 carried = 4) 48

Shortcut: 3 X 15 = 45
Then 45 + (3 X 1=3) 45 + 3 = 48
Eventually, you will do these calculations in your head

5-P

3 X 19 = 57 (3 X 9 = 27 post the 7 and carry the 2; 3 X 1 = 3
And add the carried 2 for total of 5 so answer is 57

Shortcut: 3 X 20 = 60
Then 60 minus (3 X 1 = 3)
Then 60 minus 3 = 57
Think this through and see how clever this shortcut can be.

5-Q

3 X 13 = 39
3 X 14 = 42

The difference between 39 and 42 is,
not unsurprisingly, the common 3   -- See the Pattern
3 X 15 =
3 X 16 =

5-R

The Theatre has rows of seats A to Z running from A at stage.
Each row holds 13 fold-up seats.
How many letters in the alphabet?
Calculate or state the number of floor rows to the back row.

Balcony rows of seats run AA to KK.
Calculate or state the number of balcony rows.

Calculate the Total number of seats.

Calculate the percentage of all seats on the floor to Total Seats.

Calculate the percentage of all seats in the balcony to Total Seats.

Round the percentage.

Prove your Answer.

5-S

Prices of every item and service have been rising due to the COVID-19 Pandemic and related shortages as costs of production and transportation and labor have been rising. The Russian invasion of Ukraine on February 24, 2022 has affected the global supply of goods and services. The Consumer Price Index is rising. Inflation rate has risen to 9 to 10%.

Produce price rise of 12%
Meats price rise of 27%
Dairy price rise of 15%
Paper Products price rise of 15%
Rice price rise of 35%
Gasoline price rise of 80%
Utilities price rise of 45%

Calculate the Cost of Living across-the-board average percentage price rise.

5-T

A grocery item was priced at $6. It is on sale for $4 to clear inventory. How much will we pay as a percentage? 4/6 reduced is 2/3. We have learned that 2/3 (2 divided by 3) works out to be a quotient of .666 with remainder of 2 for a percentage of 66 2/3%. So, we are enjoying a 1/3 Discount (100% is 1.00 less 66 2/3 = 33 1/3%).

Note that we get the same quotient by dividing 4 by 6 because numbers are constant.

Think and be quick to see price reductions and divide the listed amount for sale into the sale price amount to determine its percentage of the whole you would pay for the item on sale.

This is how you evaluate price before purchasing and favorably manage your higher and rising cost of living.

5-U

We are bombarded with advertisements on a daily basis. Many ads include a list price and a sale price available in a narrow window of a number of days to stimulate clearance sales of items. It is important for you to be able to figure out the amount of discount or money saved if you were to purchase the item on sale. You need to be able to think quickly and make a decision as to whether the item is worth its value to you while on sale for a lower price.

Remember how we talked about rounding up or down to make a calculation easier in your mind. Let's look at some examples:

40-inch LED TV on sale for $140. Normal price $150. Discount is $10
Discount percentage is: $10 / $150 = 6.66 or 7%% rounded up
Proof: 150 X 7% or .07 = $10.50
So, would you purchase the new-in-box for $150 to be sure the TV was untouched or purchase the sale item and save $10?

5-V

Refrigerator 17 cubic foot Retail price $929.99 or $749.99 on sale with savings of $180 (19%)

This refrigerator also on special sale called 'Open-box' for $501.99 for a savings of $428.00 or 46%.

When you look at these numbers, know that the price $929.99 is listed to lead you to believe the price is less than it is. $929.99 is really $930 and $749.99 is really $750 and $501.99 is really $502.

So, round the numbers to make it easier to see what you are looking at. When you look at the deep-discounted price of $502 you can see that it is nearly half of the retail $929 price and less than 70% of the $750 price. (Divide the rounded 500 by 750 and visualize that the quotient will be below 7 because 7 X 700 (rounded to 700) would be 4900 and see that would be too much and therefore the quotient must begin with 6)

So, in your mind you would be able to estimate that the 500 is about 60 to maybe 64% of the initial discounted price of $750. [Looking at the $500 compared to the $930 list price, it is remarkably lower and appears to be in the 40% discount range, with a reciprocal price range of 60%].

$930 X 40% = $372 discount estimate. $930 – 372 would be $558. These numbers are relative and based on estimate. The importance of estimating is to give you a quick idea leading to an action decision to purchase or not purchase.]

Let's discuss this some more. Round down the $930 to 900. Leave the $500 as $500. We know that 2 X 450 = 900. The 2 is like one-half and therefore it tells us that the amount would be near $450 rising to the $500 price we do know. Think what number times 9 (for the $900) would equal close to the $500. It would be 5. 5 X 9 = 45. So, we can estimate that the 500 is near or just less than 50% discount. Next, we can determine the amount of discount by dividing the $500 by the $930. That will give us a decimal of less than one and that will be the percentage that 500 is of 930. .53 is 53%. So, we would be paying just over 53% of the retail price.

5-W

When you see items listed for sale, think about the difference between the list price and the sale price. Quickly divide the list price into the sale price to get the quotient being less than one and being a decimal amount. Move the decimal 2 places to the right and you have the actual percentage. You can do this in your mind when you round numbers up or down to make it easier to estimate.

5-X

Grocery item is retail priced at 3 for $3.60

Calculate the average cost.

Estimate the average cost if the retail price rises by 15%

Calculate the average cost after the retail price rise.

Prove your answer.

5-Y

A $400 TV is on a one-day sale 30% off.   We know 30% is .30 decimal. Your thoughts about a quick cost calculation as an approximation would include: 30% is almost 1/3 off. So, if we multiply $400 by 1/3, we will come close to the amount of discount.

Calculate the Discount:
Calculate the net cost to purchase.

Prove your calculations.

5-Z

Bikers rode for three hours and 12 mph but the thing is that they rode over four bridges. Some hills were about 15 feet high. There was a stream. It was falling over 6 large rocks and moving at about 6 mph. Calculate how far bikers rode. Select pertinent information.

Distance = Rate X Time

5-AA

2700 representatives in 120 countries are meeting.
Calculate the average number of representatives of each country.
Round up for your answer.

5-BB

Miles and cost per mile

T drove miles during year 2021.
Mileage January 1 2021:   67,392
Mileage December 31, 2021:87,747
He logged 866 hours driving
Cost per Gallon Gas $3.37

Calculate average speed MPH   23.5
Distance = Rate X Time
Prove calculations.

5-CC

6,000 Manatees in Florida
1,000 Manatees died in Year 2021

Calculate the number of manatees that survived.
Calculate and write in fraction and percentage the number died.
Calculate and write in fraction and percentage the number alive.

1/6 (divide out to get quotient and its percentage)

5-DD

State the value and percentage of 8/8:

5-EE

Calculate number gallons of milk you purchase with $50.
Gallon milk costs $2.87

5-FF

Property is 120 feet by 80 feet
Calculate the Area in Square Feet
L x W = A

5-GG

87,747 miles reading and the
previous mileage was 87417 reading
14 gallons gas paid $1.539 per gallon
Normal gallon price is $$3.09 per gallon
Drive Time: 14 hours

Calculate Price per gallon saved:
Calculate total cost paid for gas:
Round answer if appropriate

Why is the gas cost $1.539?
What does the 9 mean to you?

Who benefits and who pays for the 9?

Calculate the Miles per Gallon:
Distance = Rate X Time

23.5

5-HH

Walked nonstop from 7:47 AM until 2:04 PM
Calculate hours and minutes walked:

8 − 2 =   4 + (60 − 47)

5-II

Drove West 533 miles to St. Louis, Missouri.
Departed at 7:13 AM.
Arrived at 4:07 PM.
2 stops of 13 minutes each.

Calculate hours in vehicle:
Calculate average speed:

Distance = Rate X Time

533

5-JJ

Business Statistics and Report

Gross Sales	2,746,561.10	100%
Cost of Goods Sold	2,304,804.92	
Gross Profit	441,756.18	
Selling and Admin Expenses	238,156.67	
Profit from Above Operations	203,599.51	
Other Revenues/Expenses (Net +)	12,295.17	
Net Taxable Profit	215,894.68	
Income Tax Provision	83,139.68	
Net Profit after income tax	132,755.00	4.8%

Calculate the percentages of Gross Sales for each line.
Round percentage up or down.
Think about these statistics and what they tell you
about running a business.

These numbers are lifted off an actual Certified Public Accountant
Annual Audit Report of a post-World War II 1946 brewery.

5-KK

We want to build a playhouse.
Time is required. Materials are required.
Common sense, knowledge and skills and abilities are required.

Considerations / Specifications:

Study and design and dimensions
Visit Supplier of needed construction materials
List materials required by dimensions and when needed
Inquire and determine schedule of needed materials availability in view
of COVID-19 Pandemic delivery limitations
Lay out the sequence of construction

Cost to dig and pour concrete footings and sand-based floor, patio, and sidewalk access
Cost to bury water line for kitchen sink with drain to French drain
Cost to bury an electric line to receptacles
Quantity and length and cost of rough lumber 2 X 4 studs required
Quantity and length and cost of joists for roof
Quantity and cost of bundles of roof shingles
Quantity and length and thickness and cost of plywood and drywall
Quantity and cost of cupboards to fit a length of wall
Quantity and cost of entry door and windows
Quantity and cost of decorative shutters
Quantity and cost of exterior wall sheeting or vinyl siding
Tarps to cover materials and work-in-progress from weather
Playhouse floor surface
Finish moldings
Tools and nails and screws
Paint for interior and exterior
Interior shelves, furniture, cushions, erasable board, decorations
Time required and items not on list
Materials Delivery Costs

Estimated materials costs Total: $3,286.58

Estimated hours cost Total: 87 hours at $24 per hour

Calculate Total Cost:
Calculate Materials percentage of Total Cost:
Calculate Hours percentage of Total Cost:

Label the four major directions on a compass.
How many degrees apart are the directions?
How many degrees are in a right-angle?
How many degrees are in a straight line?
How many degrees are in a circle?

Which compass direction is associated with Sunrise?
Which compass direction is associated with Sunset?
Are the Sunrise and Sunset directions parts of a right-angle?

When the Sun moves across the sky during the day, which direction does it move across?

What time is Sunrise and what does it mean to you?
What time is Sunset and what does it mean to you?

5-MM

Time Study

How we use our time determines how much time we have to use.

Student study day:

Activity	Minutes	%	Your Actual	%
Rise 7 AM	30			
Breakfast	20			
Class/Study	180			
Lunch	30			
Class/Study	180			
Dinner	40			
Study	60			
Social Media	360			
Bedtime 10 PM				
Sleep	540			
- Minutes				
- Hours				

The time you have to use is determined by how you use your time.

Total the minutes and convert minutes to hours.
Calculate the percentage of the day devoted to each activity.
Be bold and enter your Actual for each activity.

Look at your days this past week and think about how you might change your time allocation. Social Media is a high number.
Evaluate to determine what good value you get from Social Media.

5-NN

Read and Compare Ingredients on food items.

Dairy Milk Carton reads: 120 Calories per serving size
Dairy Milk Carton reads: Calcium 293 mg (Milligrams)

Almond Milk Carton reads: 60 Calories per serving size
Almond Milk Carton reads: Calcium 450 mg (Milligrams)

Almond Milk Carton reads: 50% More Calcium than Dairy Milk

Calculate difference in Calories between the two:

Calculate percentage of difference in Calories between the two:

Calculate to determine if Calcium Statement is correct:

Prove your calculations.

Read and understand product ingredients to your better health.

5-OO

Drove the car 433 miles on a tank of gas
Filled the tank with 15 gallons gas
Calculate the miles driven per gallon
Round answer upward

Prove your answer.

We close these challenging calculations with a look into numbers impacting every person on our planet.

Be aware of what is happening in the world and how it may affect your life. The COVID-19 Coronavirus Pandemic has been ravaging the entire world since November 2019. Statistics are important. Statistics are numbers and relationships that reveal patterns and may be the foundation of decisions about what to do and not do. Let's look at the statistics of the COVID-19 Pandemic and its two known Variants: Delta and Omicron.

Read across these numbers aloud to practice and understand.

Worldwide Population: 7 Billion 874 Million 965 Thousand 825 Eight Hundred Twenty-five or 7,874,965,825 in July 2021.

Worldwide Population: 7 Billion 973 Million 923 Thousand 276 Two Hundred Seventy-six or 7,973,923,276 in September 2022.

These numbers reflect an increase of 98,957,451or 1.256%

This total increases due to births totaling 97,671,567
and deaths totaling 41,005,178

COVID-19 Corona Virus Pandemic Statistics

Sunday, January 30, 2022

Worldwide

	Number	Percentage
Total Infected	374,679,559	100%
New Cases	1,731,380	
Recovered	295,760,572	
Active Cases	73,239,624	
Died	5,679,363	

Calculate the percentages of the Total Infected
Prove your answers are equal to or approximately 100%

United States

	Number	Percentage US	Percent of World
Total Infected	75,546,580	100%	
New Cases	65,458		
Recovered	45,918,450		
Active Cases	28,721,093		
Died	907,037		

Calculate World Wide percentages:

Calculate US percentages:

Calculate US numbers as a percentage of Worldwide numbers:

Think about what these statistics tell you and how you can use them as a step forward in your education and also as conversational topics.

--

Sunday, February 6, 2022

These are the same statistics seven days later.

Worldwide

	Number	Percentage
Total Infected	395,461,221	100%
New Cases	1,542,695	
Recovered	314,059,932	
Active Cases	75,645,545	
Died	5,755,744	

United States

	Number	Percentage US	Percent of World
Total Infected	77,972,120	100%	
New Cases	58,477		
Recovered	47,902,271		
Active Cases	29,144,147		
Died	925,702		

Calculate World Wide percentages:

Calculate US percentages:

Calculate US numbers as a percentage of Worldwide numbers:

Calculate numbers increase/decrease in 7 days:

Calculate average number increase/decrease in 7 days each line:

Calculate percentages increase/decrease for 7 days for US and Percent of World:

Consult with a mentor to review your calculations.

GRADUATION

Graduation signals a moment of acknowledging your commitment to continuing your education as a great gift to yourself by becoming a life-long learner seeking new information, to assure you are fully informed.

The purpose of this book has been to introduce yourself to yourself and to discuss how to identify, build and strengthen your relationship with *simple math* to the point that you may develop a positive attitude toward enjoying math and acknowledging the important place it plays in your present and future life.

When you are at a point of comfortableness with the concepts, formulas and mechanics of *simple math*, you will have positioned yourself with knowledge and experience under your belt. You may rely on this being a valuable asset in your knowledge toolbox. You will be pulling out this tool as it applies to various projects, or as you think and work toward a solution to a problem – or when you gift your knowledge to another.

Congratulations for having brought yourself through these exercises. You will be pleased with what you have completed and how you feel as the result of befriending *simple math*. You are prepared to continue practicing and improving your math skills.

You have learned, persevered and changed your life for the better. You owned your commitment to yourself and followed through to make it happen for yourself. You taught yourself that you are able to set your mind to something new to you and do what you decided to do to improve your life. You are better-prepared.

Remember, this is the beginning. When you begin something new, it is important that you keep it going and continue on yourself-guided path of achievement. Yes, there is more to math, and you are prepared to pursue learning much more.

Best to you as you continue to make positive choices in your life.

AFTERWORD

You have done well to reach this point in this book.
What has taken place?

You were advised up front that this book would address and share the elements of *simple math* in a workbook setting.

You have worked through the Exercises and challenges to arrive here, knowing that you have improved your math skills.

You now realize that learning can be fun. Teaching yourself simple, yet challenging, content can be fun. The right attitude makes it easy for you and even spurs you onward. You have achieved.

You are on your way to befriending *simple math* so that you may be able to more-comfortably rely on it daily. Study, think and learn, and understand and befriend the times tables and decimal equivalents.

Continue to spot opportunities to work *simple math* problems using the shortcuts so that you may master the principles and applications and techniques of *simple math*, to your best advantage.

I acknowledge your effort and diligence in sticking to these study and workbook pages. You are the beneficiary. The benefits will last you your entire life.

Best to you for developing the thrill of continued life-long learning.

R. K.

MENTOR CONVERSATION

Let's have another conversation and review   ...

As was stated, this book is dedicated to you and each other person seeking to gain insight into a new way of thinking and developing behavior patterns with the goal of effecting lasting change, a positive perspective and an improved way of life as a means of creating the present and future life desired. Give the book to someone else.

It is intended to be for your mind as a gym would be for your physical development assuring stability and agility. Your mind seeks stability and agility in solving *simple math* challenges. Mastery of math comes from practice leading to a partnership with math in your life. Your reliance on math, and its expanded integration into your daily life, will build as you realize how much you subconsciously already know and use it. Your use of math will empower you. *Simple math* offers you an opportunity for daily mental gymnastics, which strengthen your entire body system and lengthen life with a positive and meaningful attitude.

You are born with talents. You develop skills and abilities. You may couple these together with a positive Can-do attitude and an As-if behavior and reframe yourself to be who you know yourself to be, or to be whom you wish or plan yourself to be. This book is intended to help you develop your skills and abilities related to *simple math* and they will extend across your life's focus of activities.

When you dedicate yourself, by your Contract with Yourself, to learning and practicing the content shared in this book, you will improve. Your commitment to practicing creates the space for improvement to flourish. You can take the discipline of this book and apply it to all the facets of your life. You are on your road of learning. You can do this.

You become what you think about. So, be sure to think about matters and things important to you and your future. This is a simple formula leading to self-improvement in any area of your life. Silence supports learning and understanding because it gives space for clarity of thought to manifest itself. When you honor silence, you dismiss distractions.

Thinking separates us from every living creature. Computers have been developed with advanced artificial intelligence, on which you may rely for instant answers. Yet, they fail to replace thinking in your own mind and challenging yourself to pursue mental exercises to expand your knowledge, skills and abilities relative to *simple math* and your outer world. If we default to answers provided by artificial intelligence, we surrender our identity bit-by-bit until there may be little to none left. This alone, may be reason enough for you to focus on learning *simple math* as an exercise enabling your brain to serve you as intended by your Creator.

At the end of each day, you are a much better person for having been thinking and taking up the baton of learning *simple math* instead of succumbing to a false belief that it may be too much for you.

Did you ever face something in life and think it would be impossible for you to do? Do you give in to such self-limiting and negative thoughts? Yes, it may take longer for you to learn this as opposed to something else you may be more interested in. Yet, when you have mastered *simple math*, you will reap the valued rewards of self-satisfaction and having achieved what was believed to be difficult. This happens when you meet the challenge with determination and perseverance, coupled with the attitude that you will face, work through, understand and absorb the exercises and techniques to your own benefit.

You can become the best of your best when you set your mind to it. Your mind is a fertile garden waiting for the seeds of your thoughts applied to the formulas and processes of math. Your thoughts determine whether you have a bumper crop of flowers, food, or mental gymnastics leading to your enhancing your understanding and friendship with math, or just weeds as your crop. Be sure you sow the best thought seeds fertilized by a Can-do attitude for the best outcome you desire.

Reading, thinking about, studying and mastering *simple math* gives you the opportunity to upload and install new software in your brain so you may be better prepared for your new future. When you are a master and prepared, the world will appear with an opportunity you may grasp before it disappears.

Ask yourself how long you are willing to not master *simple math* and what it might cost you. Ask yourself if you are willing to forfeit an opportunity that this mastery may offer you because you will have learned and be prepared for eventualities. Stick with this study.

There is a distinct need to know and understand and befriend and enjoy the simplicity and constancy of math in your life. It is logical. It always makes sense. It will be as logical and sensible as you decide it is, or will be. It is also as complicated or difficult as you may decide it is, or will be in your life. So, decide now to get on board with further study and determine which side of the equation you are on, or going to be on.

You may find and acknowledge that math is useful to you as you reflect on how it has been silently in your life. You unconsciously let it in to help you. It is a foundation of business. Students use math. Everyone uses math. You use math. So, this book has offered an opportunity to expand your knowledge by working *simple math* practice problems and developing a discipline of consciously including math in your day. The problems and examples may bring the process into your real life and support the idea that you can master it and do it well. Examples bring the idea and process into your mind for you to work with.

Focused practice is the seed to improvement and leads to a greater understanding. Think back to when you embarked on a new adventure and how well you did. This is merely another adventure. You control the process and the outcome. You are the beneficiary of your own devotion to math. Other people master math. You can do this too, beginning right now. Inaction is an expensive decision lasting forever as a negative force in your life.

Some people play board games. Perhaps, you do. That is great. This is another avenue of mental stimulation leading to achievements.

Some people watch TV. Some wander aimlessly. Some do not know how to stimulate themselves and therefore may not know what to do. So, some do nothing. Doing nothing is doing something that gets you nowhere. When a person allows this to happen, the incentive to achieve is crushed. Make sure you avoid this pitfall.

On the contrary, you can make this a fruitful hobby and pastime leading you to think logically and become solution-oriented as a creative activity instead of idleness as a passive activity.

Rework each problem offered in sequence before looking at answers.

This book speaks to discipline as your lead to achievement as you draw closer to the finish line of your goal. Discipline serves as your roadmap. Discipline is focus on your priorities. Make this your priority. Put your mind and heart to this and you can win the elusive prize and be a Master of yourself and *simple math* and receive the achievement award as Emma, the girl to whom this book is dedicated, wishes you to do. Join her. You can do this.

Imagine how you will feel when this happens and is your new reality. You have only so much time in your life. It is up to you to decide how you will allocate your remaining time. Time assigned to personal education is well spent as it reaps a life-long benefit. You will better-enjoy your days when you have befriended *simple math*.

The choice is yours as to how you form your future. It is in your hands waiting for you to make a decision and to embrace your self-created new future.

Let's keep on thinking and preparing you for your post-graduation life!

COMMENTARY

FURTHER THOUGHTS

Let's continue to sit and have a conversation about what you just covered and learned in this book and even-more-so about your life.

Is there a sense of urgency for you to begin working on mental gymnastics? The answer is a resounding YES! There is no time like the present. When you put off doing what is good for you, the damage may never manifest itself because you may not know the difference between where you may be and where you could have moved yourself to be. Begin now.

Your ability to add, subtract, multiply and divide numbers and understand the relationship of numbers is key to mental acuity. We are constantly bombarded with information and find ourselves in situations requiring quick thinking and action. Mental gymnastics keeps us prepared. Math mental gymnastics will keep you better-prepared for when the unexpected event or occurrence takes you by surprise. We keep on learning and feeding our brain by using it and developing our minds to be sharp and alert.

You can let go of any self-limiting beliefs and feelings holding you back. When you do this, you end old ways. When you end old ways, you open yourself to a new beginning. New beginnings necessarily require an end of something the new beginning will replace. Embrace your decision for a specific end to old ways and adoption of your new beginning. You are prepared for this. Keep on keeping on now.

HABIT

A habit is a pattern of behavior formed after we do something or think a certain way for three to six weeks. The time frame differs by individual and is determined by variables of consideration or persistence in the formation of the habit until it becomes second nature. That means it becomes automatic. Your brain will have adopted it as normal for you. Develop the habit of thinking about how to apply *simple math* to whatever you are doing.

When walking, think of what you are doing instead of listening to music or other input. That is not to say that listening to music is not beneficial. It is. When I was a junior in high school, I wrote a term paper titled "Music, the International Language." Little did I know how true that would be proven to be. Look at today, when the music of all sources and countries is appreciated across all borders. What I mean to say is that when you are developing a habit of attending to math and how it impacts daily life and your future, it is important that you tune out other distractions so that you will be able to focus for the time being on developing math as an integral part of your consciousness.

This book is a Do-it-Yourself for you and whomever will support you. It may help you teach yourself how to learn. It may help you to develop and embrace a self-discipline regime otherwise new to you. That may be good for you. That is for you to determine.

Know that when you work these math exercises out with someone else and talk about the process and your understanding of it, the challenge is cut more than in half for you. So, ask someone to help you with this process to make it easier for you and more meaningful. Another person helps you to get to the finish line. Your finish line is also a measurement. Most everything has or is a measurement.

EXERCISES

The exercises are tools for you to work through to a valued outcome.
You determine the strength and place value on the outcome.
You had to think carefully about each exercise, and how it comes
together and figure out what it teaches you about numbers and begin to
see how it can fit into your life.

The exercises set a pace for you. Slow and steady, like the turtle, will
win the race/prize. Review and re-devote yourself to five days of each
exercise so that it cements in your mind. Think of the one exercise
before you at a time. Let it sink in. Think about it when you are doing
other things. That brings clarity to confusion. Thinking is magical. The
results last your lifetime.

Thinking breeds understanding, which provides a foundation on which
to build the next exercise. You have to apply yourself and stick to it to
reach the other side of knowledge about any subject. Again, this is a
subject that will serve you your entire life. Focus now with the goal of
re-celebrating your graduation.

It takes five fingers to pick up a handful of gravel. Likewise, it will take
your deliberate completion of each of the five exercises to befriend
math and let it be a new part of you, on which you may not-only-rely,
but actually enjoy. The expression of the five fingers picking up gravel is
a metaphor representing your completion of the five exercises.
Your completion of the five exercises represents your complete hand
with five fingers able to pick up the gravel. In the case of math, the five
exercises enable you to go on in life prepared to address the situations
in which *simple math* arise in your daily life, because you will have in
your hand (brain) the ability to think, assimilate and solve problems.

WHY DO YOU BOTHER?

We befriend numbers and math because they are an integral part of daily living. We depend on numbers and their uses for determining answers.

We use numbers for:

Taxes on real estate - calculation monthly, annual or for five years
Time
Recording sunrise, sunset and noon
Knowing when to leave and allow sufficient time to arrive at destination
Age
Size
Length
Distance
Quantity
House address numbers
Currency
Wages
Taxes
Accounting and bookkeeping amounts
Sales
Costs
Estimating
Approximating
In meetings
In traffic
Studying
Assuring adequate time for sleep
License Numbers
Street numbers
House Mortgage
Temperature in Centigrade or Fahrenheit
Wind-chill factor
Consumer Price Index
Inflation
Paint color numbers

Product model numbers
UPC Number Codes on products
Tire sizes
Weights
Ingredients
Symbols
Statistics
Square foot
Square yard
Depth of water
Measure of size, length, width and height and weight
Comparisons
Gallons
Liquid measure
Powder measure
Volume
Airplane flight numbers
Schedule time for plane, bus, train, taxi, awakening, bedtime, lunch
meals, meetings, work day
Fuel tank capacity
Capacity of vehicles of all sorts
Construction measurement is 16-inch on center for studs for drywall
Calculate number of bricks to purchase to build building
Rows in a garden
Streets
Blocks in a city
Traffic lights
Vehicles, boats
Passengers in transportation: plane, ship, taxi, truck, bus
Rooms in house
Floors in building
Height of ceiling
Tires in storeroom
Employees in department store
Wrenches on shelf
Pounds of air in a tire
Bicycle riders in park
Number of seats in picnic gazebo, car, bus, airplane, train

The above list is limited and merely an example.

We use numbers and math so much that it may be easier to identify when we do not use numbers and math instead of list when we do. Because numbers and math are ever-present in your daily life, decide now to learn how to integrate them into your thinking for a better understanding of life. The discipline they offer you will manifest itself when you live according to the logical principles of math.

NUMBERS

Here are other thoughts about numbers for you to think about.
These are practical incidents of persons using simple math, just as the exercises gave you a view of day-to-day problems to solve.

Numbers are everywhere. Numbers work in every language. Numbers are used for measurements in every language. Measurements work everywhere.

We see numbers or measurements of hillsides; altitude; in the depths of the ocean; in census counts; construction. *Simple math* numbers work every place for everybody. That's why I tell you that they are constants.

So, we rely on them and measure and use numbers and what they can do for us. Numbers are precise.

You will be the person who will master *simple math*. Your mastery will gradually come to you. Practice makes improvement.

What you find out is that it is *simple math* that you use most of the time and that's what most other people use most of the time. We are not talking about the complex math of professionals. *Simple math* is the foundation on which complex math is formulated.

The cement contractor who is laying the 3-foot-wide sidewalk uses constant measurements to make the slabs equal and pour them together so that they make a sidewalk of a given thickness. Same thing is true for concrete roadways or football stadiums or asphalt roadways. They all get laid out and we do see pre-construction surveys and plans taking place to determine measurements. We see survey marker stakes that are used as guidelines and they provide the corners of property or the curbs in the property or in the road or otherwise.

A contractor was introducing underground cabling. He had to measure and know the distance between his input and output points so that the crew would know how long of a cable would be required for insertion to accomplish the project. Likewise, they also need to know what the weight and diameter dimensions would be for connecting the cable to another cable. So, you see that the uses of *simple math* provide an opportunity and knowledge for doing things right the first time. That reduces the probability and expense of mistakes.

When there is a need to determine how many wheelbarrows of slag or gravel or topsoil would be required to cover a certain space to a certain depth, then we're talking about length times width times the depth or the height and that will give you the cubic feet fill that is required. This is *simple math* being applied.

Measurements are used in sports. When you watch a football game, you see that the ball could end up 1 inch from a new down or a first down or a fourth down and that could be a turning point in the game. The distance is measured on the sideline of the field. Likewise, when a basketball or soccer ball shoot misses the net by an inch or if a football on a goal is kicked and it hits a goal post and it misses by an inch, there's no score. Scores are numbers representing an achievement.

So, we see that the use of measurements and incremental measurements is on a daily basis and across all activities from elements in your personal life through to sports, engineering, maintenance, contracting and just *simple math* that you're using in order to calculate how many boxes of cereal may be eaten to feed a certain group.

Another example may be that you hear you have 150 people to be fed and that there is an average that we have to calculate to be sure the food gets to each person. If there is an average of 10 servings in each box then how many boxes of cereal will be required to give cereal to each of the 150 guests? Calculate this in your head.

If you're in a business and you're in the process of serving people in a restaurant, then you have to know what is your capacity so that you don't exceed that for fire code safety reasons. You have to know you are doing your best to keep your customers safe by complying with occupancy and fire safety guidelines.   Also, numbers are important to know because if you have open seating on the inside and you get a phone call asking whether you could serve a group of 82, and you have 150 as your capacity, then it would be important at that moment for you to count the number of individuals in the restaurant, or waiting to be seated, in order to subtract that number from the capacity to know whether or not you can say yes to the phone caller that you can handle 82 new customers coming in at that very moment and still remain in compliance with the fire code standards of occupancy. Numbers are constants that serve you and numbers work everywhere.

Graphs provide a picture of a pattern or a trend by comparing two or more values. They include relative data and values. The purpose of a graph is to make data and information visually understandable. Devote your time and attention to reviewing the graphic presentations you come across and think of what it tells. See the couple below. Think.

NUMBERS IN BUSINESS REPORTS AND ARTICLES

Percentages fill the pages of writings about the economy and global businesses and help with understanding what is happening.

For example: The price of nickel has risen from US $4.50 per pound in 2016 to around US $10 per pound, about 167 percent above the 10-year moving average, according to a BMO Capital Markets.

Another Headline: On November 15, 2021[1] "President Biden signed the biggest infrastructure-spending bill of all time. A staggering $226

BILLION is earmarked for projects REQUIRING huge amounts of copper."

"Copper has skyrocketed 79% from February 2020 to February 2022[2] and many experts believe this is only the beginning of a massive bull run for this shiny metal.

Turns out, copper is a desperately needed mineral to power the green revolution of clean emission-free energy.

And Joe Biden has just given copper and its investors a huge boost. That's because The Infrastructure Investment and Jobs Act of 2021[3] is like a shopping list of copper-based projects backed by a $226 billion government gift card.

Biden has NO CHOICE but to throw hundreds of billions behind copper if he has any hope of delivering on the promise for a clean energy future."

"President Biden aims to make EV (Electric Vehicles) switch easier, approves funding for EV charging infrastructure"
Thu, September 15, 2022 at 11:52 AM
Yahoo Finance's Pras Subramanian breaks down President Biden's announcement on electric vehicle infrastructure funding.

JOE BIDEN: "So today, I'm pleased to announce we're approving funding for the first 35 states-- including Michigan-- to build their own electric charging infrastructure throughout their state.
[CROWD CHEERING]
And y'all are going to be part of a network of 500,000 charging stations.
- We have Pras Subramanian here to discuss more on this. Pras says: And we just heard from President Biden it's $900 million in grants. What do you make of this announcement? And does it really move the needle here just in terms of EV adoption down the road?
PRAS SUBRAMANIAN: Yeah. You know, it's the big, kind of, continuation of this plan to spend $7.5 billion building out this whole charging network across the nation's highways. You mentioned 35 states, now, are going to have this-- almost, I think, 53,000 miles of highway is going to be covered by this network. And it's going to cost, Andy mentioned there, $900 million."

Copper was one of the first metals ever extracted and used by humans, and it has made vital contributions to sustaining and improving society since the dawn of civilization. Copper is an excellent conductor of electricity. Most copper mined today is used to conduct electricity - mostly as wiring. It is also an excellent conductor of heat and is used in cooking utensils, heat sinks, and heat exchangers. Large amounts are also used to make alloys such as brass (copper and zinc) and bronze (copper, tin, and zinc). Copper is also alloyed with precious metals such as gold and silver. Copper is easily stretched, molded, and shaped; is resistant to corrosion; and conducts heat and electricity efficiently. As a result, copper was important to early humans and continues to be a material of choice for a variety of domestic, industrial, and high-technology applications today. Presently, copper is used in building construction, power generation and transmission, electronic product manufacturing, and the production of industrial machinery and transportation vehicles. Copper wiring and plumbing are integral to the appliances, heating and cooling systems, and telecommunications links used every day in homes and businesses. Copper is an essential component in the motors, wiring, radiators, connectors, brakes, and bearings used in cars and trucks.

Copper supply is falling into deficit status with demand exceeding the projected or actual supply. As a result of the COVID-19 Pandemic coupled with the long-term Pandemic-related closure of economic activity on a global basis and the Russian invasion of neighboring Ukraine on February 24, 2022, the demand for and the price for copper and other commodities has crashed.

Copper has long been recognized as a bellwether because its demand and supply forces signal economic health and/or changes.

Copper is a key commodity raw material in demand across the globe. As the commitment to transition from fossil fuels to electric power takes hold and goals are set to achieve benchmarks in the transition, copper will become even more important due to its conductivity and flexibility as well as because it is used in all industries and businesses.

The graph below shows volume of demand and the color coding reflects the Country or Region. Study the chart for what it might tell you.

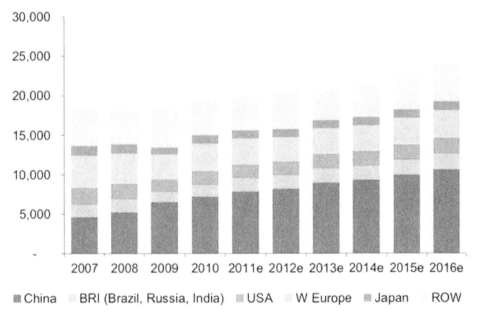

Copper Demand by Region

(Global refined demand, MT/year)

Source: WMBH, Morgan Stanley Commodity Research estimates

--

ROW means Rest of the World

Here is a graph illustrating Copper pricing since January 2000 and Yahoo! Finance is again credited:

--

--

This Yahoo! Finance quote and graph dated Thursday September 15, 2022 pictures the 12-years' fluctuations in the price of copper since September 01, 2000, when it sat at $0.64. Six years passed before it rose to $3.63 on September 1, 2007. It was $3.93 on April 1, 2008. Then it crashed to $1.39 on December 1, 2008. It stayed in the deep trough for a month and rose to $1.46 January 1, 2009. Then there was a slow and arduous climb up to $4.43 December 1, 2010. Then the price gradually fell to $2.06 on January 1, 2016. The fall was a 53% drop and a loss for investors as demand fell off a cliff bringing the price crashing down. By December 1, 2017, there was a modest rise back to the $3.27 level. This was followed by another drop to the price level of $2.35 on April 1, 2020. This was still the beginning of COVID and demand throttled the price to a dramatic rise to $4.568 on May 1, 2021. Then demand fell off a cliff as the global economy struggled with supply issues and falling production reducing the need for raw materials. On Thursday September 15, 2022 Copper is priced at $3.4925 per pound.

--

Look at this information and read the graph and match it to the above text and understand what was just discussed.

--

President Biden's decisions will touch the lives of every American because the demand for copper will outstrip the supply. Supply and demand will come into play and force the price higher as supply diminishes. Watch for future discussions and charts about this as the President's September 14, 2022 announcement at the 2022 Detroit Auto Show takes hold.

The top bar on the Yahoo! Finance page for copper reflected daily ever-changing figures and performance marks like is illustrated below. These are key financial standards you may wish to explore for the valuable information hidden in the numbers. Below you see the value at the moment, the change and the percentage of change. Think. The links are active links filled with information for you on Yahoo! Finance.

S&P 500	Dow 30	Nasdaq	Nasdaq
3,939.89	31,230.77	11,685.20	11,687.01
		-34.48(-	-32.67(-
-6.12(-0.16%)	+95.68(+0.31	0.29%)	0.28%)

Russell 2000	Crude Oil	Gold
1,841.10	85.56	1,676.40
	-2.92(-	
+2.63(+0.14%)	3.30%)	-32.70(-1.91%)

Below is a chart reporting important information releases. Major policy and economic decisions are based on these elements of information.

Notice the timing. The releases are timed to allow the US Economic managers and those in the global market to absorb the status presented.

--

Today's Economic Releases
Thursday, September 15, 2022

	United States	Reference Date	Value	Previous	Units
9:15 AM	Capacity Utilization	Aug 2022	79.96	80.2	%, SA
9:15 AM	Industrial Production	Aug 2022	104.55	104.72	Index 2017=100, SA
7:00 AM * _	Stock Market Index	14 Sep 2022	31,135	31,104	Index 26May1896=40.94, NSA
4:15 PM * _	Average Long-term Government Bond	14 Sep 2022	N/A	3.42	% p.a., NSA
4:15 PM * _	Lending Rate	14 Sep 2022	N/A	2.33	% p.a., NSA
4:15 PM *	Money Market Rate	Sep 2022	N/A	2.33	% p.a., NSA
4:15 PM * _	Treasury Bills (over 31 days)	14 Sep 2022	N/A		

This is but the top of the list intended to give you an idea of the information available as well as how it may be presented.

The Finance section of a newspaper or of on-line presentations provide you with a plethora of opportunities to use *simple math* as you read and understand the discussions. Take advantage of this wealth of information and think about it and how it may apply to your life and you will be a more-knowledgeable person for it.

R K

--

ECONOMICS

Economics is the story of the economy of the United States and, logically, the economies of the global community of countries because the economies of the various countries are inter-related more-so now because the global supply chains link businesses and fiancé across borders.

Originally, communities and countries were self-sustaining in that what was needed was produced and consumed locally. This resulted in an economic circle where the producers and consumers were the same persons.

Today, it is most important to look at the global community and create and maintain a balanced approach to economic relationships because countries today do not produce solely what they consume. Hence, we know that all countries import food and goods. Likewise, for that to be true, each country produces more than what may be consumed within its borders. So, each country exports - sells and ships out to other countries foods, goods and services.

Earlier we discussed and looked at a few examples of inflation, which is when the prices of goods and services rises and the purchasing power of the local currency is unable to purchase the same amount of goods and services for the same price. Therefore, purchasers pay more for less.

Governments take steps to curtail the rise in prices and the cost of living as a result of inflation. The United States Federal Reserve Bank possesses authority to adjust interest rates to accelerate the economy by making it easier with low interest rates for the purchasers and sellers to do business and support the economy.

The balance we witness today at the beginning of October 2022 is that The Federal Reserve is raising interest rates to tame the economy. What this means is that as interest rates rise, the cost of doing business rises and those costs add to the price of goods on the shelf so purchasers pay more for the goods purchased. When this happens, purchasers pull back on their volume of purchases and the economy slows and the radical price rises slow as the economy slows.

The Federal Reserve Central Bank's economic triggers exist similarly in the Central Banks of each country. Each country is now dealing with inflation and attempting to guide the economy to reduce the effect of inflation on the cost of living on a daily basis for citizens. The higher the interest rate rises, the greater the risk that the slowing of the economy may have a downward momentum that may or could drive the economy into a recession. A recession is when economic activity in a particular country or economy enters a period of economic decline, with trade and industrial activity producing goods becoming slowed and reduced. When this pattern in the US results in the US Gross Domestic Product of goods and services produced falls for two successive quarters, a recession rears its ugly head. The United States is close to a recession as I write. Evidence of a recession is seen in reduced economic activity resulting in lay-offs or discharges of employees, higher unemployment and a marked reduction in production and related consumer spending.

This is where the Federal Reserve attempts to maintain a balance of higher interest rates to slow the economy while not throwing economic activity into a downward spiral resulting in a recession.

As the Federal Reserve raises the US interest rates in progressive steps, this higher interest rate draws investor money from outside the US because the US interest rate is higher. Today the US interest rate has strengthened the value of the US Dollar because everyone wants the US Dollar and so it is in demand. When this happens during an inflationary period, the value of other currencies falls and people want to own safe and desired US Dollars instead of their own country currency.

Below is a table showing what has happened as a result of the strengthening of the United States Dollar as compared to other currencies across the globe.

Change in Currency Values Against the US Dollar

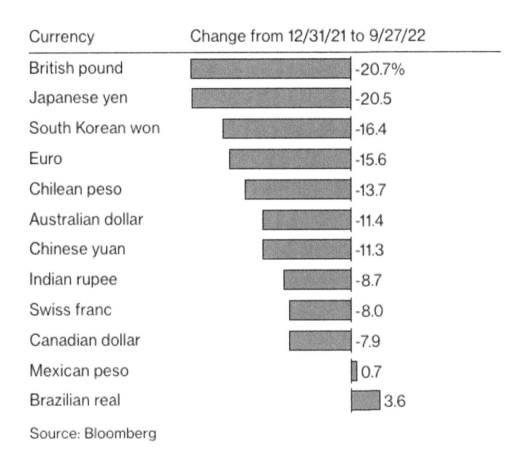

Currency	Change from 12/31/21 to 9/27/22
British pound	-20.7%
Japanese yen	-20.5
South Korean won	-16.4
Euro	-15.6
Chilean peso	-13.7
Australian dollar	-11.4
Chinese yuan	-11.3
Indian rupee	-8.7
Swiss franc	-8.0
Canadian dollar	-7.9
Mexican peso	0.7
Brazilian real	3.6

Source: Bloomberg

This table suggests that the strong US Dollar has had a reverse effect on the other currencies because they are devalued. This is true. Yet the value of a devalued currency is lost in an inflationary environment because it is favorable to exports, yet because the global economy is experiencing the same economic malaise, finding buyers for exports has become challenging because global buyers are in decline due to higher costs they face as result of inflation across-the-board.

The decline in the value of the other countries' currencies has the contrary effect of increasing the cost of imported foods and goods while also hampering the stimulation of the national economic cycle and growth.

The economic problems in other countries become exacerbated because the desire is to raise interest rates to bring the currency more up-to-par with the US Dollar and this is attempted at the risk of creating the danger of a downward spiral in economic activity resulting in a recession in those countries also.

The effect of the Federal Reserve interest rate hikes on the US economy spill over onto the inter-connected global economy because what happens to the US Dollar dramatically affects the value of other currencies, as we saw in the above chart.

The Federal Reserve will attempt to harness inflation with higher interest rates bringing about a higher cost of money borrowed as well as higher costs of living for everyone, to slow the economy while watching closely to balance that with signals that the economy has slowed enough and is close-to and not-yet-in recession before moderating the interest rates lower in order to provide minimal stimulus to economic activity, while not allowing a quick economic recovery, which may result in inflation again. The point of adjustment in interest rates downward may be when the rate of inflation has fallen from its high to around 2%. That is a long fall and it will probably take a year during which the economy will be struggling and we will see increased employee lay-offs and higher unemployment due to lower economic activity and higher inflation costs, and finally a steadying in price tags for consumers and a more-positive economic outlook.

Be aware that the actual unemployment rate may be much higher than statistics report. This is because many unemployed for a long period of time may fall off the unemployed ranks and not be counted though they may have been unsuccessful in securing renewed employment.

So, for these people, the effects of unemployment last a long time because they drop out of the work force and may accept less and struggle, or take lower-paid jobs and never recover

The Federal Reserve governors are concerned about this hidden fact when they deal with tradeoffs, just as we do in our daily lives. Yet our tradeoffs affect us, while their tradeoff decisions affect everyone.

To recap, inflation has been persistently high. It affects businesses and consumers, alike. Prices have been rising on an accelerating basis. To get prices under control, the Federal Reserve believes demand has to cool in the economy. In order to get demand to cool, the Federal Reserve is pulling the levers of assessing higher interest rates to tighten financial conditions, which makes it more expensive for businesses and consumers to finance anything. Tighter financial conditions include higher interest rates, a stronger dollar, and usually lower public stock investment valuations in the stock market.

--

On October 11, 2022, Reuters reported that "the International Monetary Fund warned that the colliding pressures from inflation, [The Russian February 24, 2022 invasion of neighboring Ukraine and the resulting war continuing – Editorial] war-driven energy and food crises and sharply higher interest rates were pushing the world to the brink of recession and threatening financial market stability.

Take note that this is the International Monetary Fund concerned about a global recession and instability in most economies and their financial markets. This is a serious statement. You would be well to take heed.

In gloomy reports issued at the start of the first in-person International Monetary Fund (IMF) and World Bank annual meetings in three years, the IMF urged central banks to keep up their fight against inflation despite the pain caused by monetary tightening and the rise in the U.S. dollar to a two-decade high, the two main drivers of a recent bout of financial market volatility."

Cutting its 2023 global growth forecasts further, the IMF said in its World Economic Outlook that countries representing a third of world output could be in recession next year.

"The three largest economies, the United States, China and the euro area, will continue to stall," Pierre-Olivier Gourinchas, the IMF's chief economist, said in a statement. "In short, the worst is yet to come, and for many people, 2023 will feel like a recession."

The IMF said Global GDP growth next year will slow to 2.7%, compared to and down from its July forecast of 2.9%, as higher interest rates slow the U.S. economy, Europe struggles with spiking gas prices and China contends with continued COVID-19 lockdowns and a weakening in property and industrial productivity sectors.

--

What this tells you is that there is an economic puzzle struggle taking place as governments'   central banks attempt to slow economies gently with the intention of avoiding the believed-around-the-corner recession.
There are unexpected contradictions taking place and these create scenarios to be handled in concert with the global changes taking place. The balance is an elusive goal. The risk is raising interest rates too quickly to cool or slow the economy and at the same time taking steps to prevent a joint stock market and bond market collapse. The expected rising rate of unemployment is looming on the horizon. As business slows, revenue and profits fall and costs rise. The cost of employees is a labor cost to be reduced by layoffs, which become more popular business changes when fewer employees are needed to sustain a declining business volume due to a recession. These snowball effects slow the economy more and may send it spiraling downward instead of allowing for a soft landing, which is an expression of what an airplane does when it lands at an airport. An economic hard landing is tough to avoid because, when the tightening of the economy by raising interest rates, resulting in money being more expensive to borrow for business or personal use, results in a quick downturn in economic activity, the

downturn is hard to stop and this results in the hard landing and a long-term recession may be the resulting economic condition.

Given the global economic environment, you may expect that we may be poised to enter a protracted recession because the sustained inflation must be brought down at all costs, or else it may destroy the global economy of many countries because they are now inter-related. Undoubtedly, there will be many persons filing for bankruptcy because they are facing the fact that they have high debts and no income and no money to pay the debts. This problem is exacerbated by the Federal Reserve's progressive raising of the interest rate in order to control inflation and its effects on each individual, business and eventually the government as the cost of money rises in direct proportion to the rising interest rate. The same exposure to the rising interest rate sequence is felt by small businesses and even large corporations because they carry the cost of debt exposure as an expense of business. When their business volume declines and they have a downturn in the sales and revenue flow of cash coming into the business, they become strapped for cash to pay short-term bills and therefore have less cash to pay off long-term debt. This may give rise to the need to borrow at the higher interest rates to stay in business. The cost of the higher interest rates may be much too high a cost and push an otherwise good business into insolvency, which means that the business has no cash to pay bills and employees and may be forced to file for bankruptcy, which means that the business files for legal protection and surrenders the valued assets of the company to be sold at liquidation prices to pay off the debts against a proportional formula. Rarely are all debts paid off. Therefore, creditors or debt-holders lose.

The economic cycle rises and falls. This pattern is natural. The Federal Reserve's Federal Open Market Committee (FOMC) meets and takes action to balance the economy much the same as we balance ourselves on a bicycle so we do not lose control and crash and experience damage. The Committee coordinates with other elements of the Federal Reserve. One works with banks and determines the discount rate and another determines the reserve requirements of banks. The coordination focuses on an economic balance to enable a best-functioning economy, or a non-functioning economy in trouble with plans to pull itself out of its possible free-fall.

The economic signs all signal the high probability that the Federal Reserve Committee will continue to raise interest rates to bring down and reduce this high inflation, which is stealing your purchasing power by making everything cost more.   We see that interest rates are now at 3 to 4% and mortgage rates are at 7%. These high interest rates will cause buyers to not enter into contracts to purchase items on credit. That will slow down the economic activity.

We witness soaring energy prices for electric and heating; the availability and high cost of food and staples in stores remains a constant challenge; maintenance and transportation costs for vehicles and trucks are rising; the reduced availability of rental space and the prices for rental space are increasing and squeezing people out of the rental market; and the home building and buying market is being squeezed as mortgage rates revisit 7% and possibly higher. The bottom line is that, across the board the cost of living is rising, such that people have run out of money. Price rises ranging across goods and services of 12% to 40% have reduced the amount of money every person may have and certainly prompts cuts in desired-and-not-needed goods and services because discretionary cash is not available in households and businesses.

My concern is that, history leaves tracks, and repeats itself and shows that prices raised due to inflation do not, or rarely, fall back down to the pricing structure pre-inflation. Persistent inflation will be with us and affect our cost-of-living for perhaps a year or even several years now. During that period, the Federal Reserve will be monitoring key economic metrics to determine how the economy is slowing and remaining stable. This inflation matter will take the 'tincture of time' to bring under control.

So, you may well expect that the higher cost-of-living we are experiencing will stay with us even when the Federal Reserve brings inflation down to its goal of 2 percent, coupled with maintaining an increase in employment as businesses become revived and hiring resumes. A low rate of inflation, along with high employment and stable prices for goods and services, serves to provide a buffer in the event of a slow-down in the economic activity of the country so that the Federal Reserve will be able to make minor adjustments to counteract a low point in economic activity in order to maintain the desired balance with the intent of avoiding deflation, which is the opposite of inflation. Deflation is as undesirable as inflation because it slows economic activity, as demand for goods and services slows, and results in higher unemployment and a temporary lowering of prices until the economy resumes its normal healthy cycle. On a peaks-and-valleys graph, inflation is high on the peak and deflation is low on the points of the valley on the graph. You may have noticed that I have emphasized that demand is a key motivator to the restoration of an economic cycle.

It is important for you to be aware of this economic information because it directly affects your daily life and helps you to understand what is happening in the United States and globally. Your awareness of the possible scenarios my help you to better-prepare for a radical economic downturn and protect yourself in the event the economy sours.

Best to you in these turbulent times when every dollar will count for you and your use of *simple math* may become more frequent as you make decisions and take steps to assure your survival.

You may observe that many people may just go ahead and pay the higher costs because they will not let the economy change their spending habits for items they want, though the items may not be needed. Steel yourself from those kinds of decisions. The time may already be here when you have to separate needs from wants.

~~~~~~~~~~~~~~~~

REAL ESTATE MORTGAGE OR SHORT-TERM LOAN

Interest is paid for the use of other-people's-money. In most cases, funds are borrowed from a business providing secured loans. An example of a secured loan is a mortgage. Household goods such as appliances and furniture may be secured for a short-term loan.

A mortgage is a long-term loan agreement enabling a buyer to purchase a home and pay off the purchase price over time. The lender may claim the property for non-payment of the mortgage.

Example: $100,000 Residence; Down Payment $10,000; Thirty-year fixed rate Interest of 7%; Private Mortgage Insurance may be required due to low down payment; Monthly Mortgage Payment around $700 paid against the principal amount of your loan – added to which would be the interest, prorated property taxes and insurance of $100 monthly.

There is a guideline that no more than 28% of your monthly total income should be obligated and paid out for a mortgage.

Amortization is a calculation by which an up-front cost or a loan is evenly spread across a certain period of time. It shows the amounts in each payment allocated for loan principal and loan interest within the scheduled monthly payment. The greater amount of payment pays interest on the loan for more than half of the term on years with a much lower amount applied to the interest portion of the payment. Many homeowners, with a 30-year mortgage, report having paid out cash in a total amount about three times the purchase price of the home over the term of the mortgage. As the amount applied to principal declines, the amount applied to interest increases late in the payment schedule.

DEBT FINANCING - AMORTIZATION

Amortization is a process and pattern by which regular payments are financed, which means to pay off a debt or loan over a certain period of time. An amortization table begins with the Principal Amount of the

Loan times the interest rate. A home mortgage is an agreement and commitment between buyer and financing agent to establish a sequence of payments to pay primarily loan interest up-front with initial payments accruing a minimal amount toward paying off the principal amount of the loan.

An amortization table details the agreement and the results of the monthly performance as prescribed. The table pictured below is one for retirement of a debt with interest. An amortization table for a home mortgage will most often include another element in the payment in addition to Interest and Principal. That other element may be a bundling of required escrow for taxes, private mortgage insurance necessary if a down payment against the purchase price is less than 20% of the purchase price. The 20% factor is believed to be sufficient investment of the buyer to bring the mortgage to completion. Additionally, there may be certain fees and closing costs, which may be rolled into the mortgage.

--

AMORTIZATION TABLE

Loan $10,000

Month of Payment	Payment Amount Constant	Interest Rate Constant	Loan Balance Declining	Interest Paid Declining	Principal Paid Increasing	Proof
1	650	0.05	10000	500	150	650
2	650	0.05	9850	492.5	157.5	650
3	650	0.05	9692.5	484.63	165.38	650
4	650	0.05	9527.13	476.36	173.64	650
5	650	0.05	9050.77	452.54	197.46	650
6	650	0.05	8598.23	429.91	220.09	650
7	650	0.05	8378.14	418.91	231.09	650

8	650	0.05	8147.05	407.35	242.65	650
9	650	0.05	7904.4	395.22	254.78	650
10	650	0.05	7649.62	382.48	267.52	650
11	650	0.05	7382.1	369.11	280.89	650
12	650	0.05	7101.21	355.06	294.94	650
13	650	0.05	6806.27	340.31	309.69	650
14	650	0.05	6496.58	324.83	325.17	650
15	650	0.05	6171.41	308.57	341.43	650
16	650	0.05	5829.98	291.5	358.5	650
17	650	0.05	5471.48	273.57	376.43	650
18	650	0.05	5095.05	254.75	395.25	650
19	650	0.05	4699.81	234.99	415.01	650
20	650	0.05	4284.8	214.24	435.76	650

			Totals	7406.8	5593.2	
					13000	proof
			20 x 650 =			
10/4/22			13000		13000	

--

As we look at this Amortization Table, we may see that in 20 months the borrower will have paid $13,000 against the $10,000 loan. The additional $3,000 is exposure to the payor for the advance use of the initial $10,000 loan.

We may note that in month 18, it appears that half of the loan has been paid off ($5,095) while the interest paid equals $6,957). These numbers show you that it is extremely expensive to borrow money to purchase something or do something. Note that this example interest rate is at 5%. That means that every month you will pay $0.05 per dollar interest on the declining balance of your loan. That means that you are paying the 5% repeatedly on the same dollars remaining throughout the term of the loan payments period. So, you see it is not that you are paying a flat rate of 5% on the loan amount, as you might think at first blush. Look at the columns and see that most of the early payments (all payments are $650) pay interest with very little of each payment going to pay off the principal amount of the loan you can see that in monthly payment number 14, the $650 payment is split nearly evenly between interest ($324.83) and Principal ($325.17). At that point, the allocation of payment between interest and principal reverses and the up-front interest payment portion begins to decline.

When you understand this discussion, you can see why loan companies are profitable because it becomes obvious that they earn their greatest profits on a loan in its early months.

Think about this discussion before obligating yourself to borrowing money or incurring credit card debt interest costs on purchases you may not really need.

This example is based on a low rate of interest of 5%. The interest rates today, in October 2022, have risen due to inflation and the interest rate increases of the Federal Reserve Bank for the purpose of tamping down inflation and slowing the economy by raising the cost of borrowing money to finance anything.

A 30-year fixed rate mortgage rate may be 6.5% or greater, depending on a credit score of 740+ and 20% of the purchase price as a down payment to assure the lender that the purchaser is invested in the property and the loan.

The interest rate charged by a loan or financing company for a quick short-term loan ranges between 15% and 20% based on the credit performance of the receiver of the loan and the risk/reward terms of the lender. Some lenders may assess loan-origination fees ($50 to $75) effectively as up-front hidden interest - raising the initial cost of the loan.

Be aware of the expensive cost of using other-people's-money.

RK

BONUS CHALLENGE CALCULATIONS

Here are random problems typical to those you may face daily.
Read, analyze for important elements of information and think.

B-1 Two vehicles are traveling at 55 MPH and collide head-on.
Calculate the speed at which the two vehicles collide.

PERCENTAGE OF PROBABILITY

B-2 Battery of a cell phone or computer reports 100% strength, battery
life and durability. As the cell phone or computer battery is used and
ages, the battery life diminishes and may recede to perhaps 80%.
When this happens, the 80% becomes the new 100% as the remaining
life after full re-charge may be only the 80% even when the battery-life
symbol reports fully charged.

B-3 Election votes are reported in whole numbers and then as a
percentage of the whole. It may be reported that 48% of the votes were
won by a certain candidate. This means that 48 of every 100 votes cast
were won by that certain candidate.

B-4 Meteorologists and Weather Reporters assign a percentage of
probability to weather patterns and expected future events within a
certain period of time. We witness this with respect to humidity (81%)
reporting the amount of water in the air, with it being at or just below
100% when rainfall is present; precipitation (rainfall) 15% meaning there
is a low possibility of rainfall; temperature within a range of a certain
number of degrees; weather forecast may identify patches of possible

rainclouds and assign a percentage of probability that a particular area may or may not receive rainfall within a time frame.

B-5 Automotive dealers have a certain number of vehicles on the sales lot. The dealers do not own the vehicles. The financing of those vehicles in inventory is called floor plan financing. New vehicles are financed with credit or a short-term loan, granted on the security of a certain vehicle in inventory, providing the dealer a certain term of months to pay the manufacturer or loan company for having vehicles available for quick sale to a buyer. The dealer has to balance the cost of having new inventory available with the cost of business, which includes the cost of financing the loan until a vehicle is sold and the loan, plus interest on that vehicle, may be paid off.

Dealers incur a daily interest cost for unsold vehicles on the sales lot. That is why we see certain vehicles advertised at a discounted price. The vehicle may have built up an obligation for interest payable for the month totaling $1,100. The vehicle needs to be sold. Advertising a discounted price provides an incentive during a narrow window of days for buyers to come and purchase. This brings in buyers willing to purchase and save $500 on an instant buy. Result: the dealer sells the vehicle for $500 less and is able to save an additional month of $1,100 interest due on the floor plan for the vehicle. Plus, the dealer sold the vehicle for $38,000 and provided cash needed now in the business operation.

Calculate the percentage of savings for the dealer.

$500 divided by $1,100 =

Calculate the percentage of the original sales price as discount to see the low cost incurred to make the $38,000 sale.

$600 divided by $38,500 =

Certainly, you may see the logic of the advertising and the effect of the low discount bringing in a sale. This is one approach a dealer uses to sell inventory.

~~~~~~~~~~~~~~~~~

INFLATION

We experience inflation in our economy or witness it in the global economy when the prices of goods and services rises. It results in a lowering of the purchasing power of money. This especially affects any person living on a fixed income because as prices rise, a certain amount of money will buy less products and services and people have to decide to do with less or without certain items or services.

Daily economic reports tell the story of price increases of food items, durable goods, clothing, paper products, lumber, machines, admission prices, utilities of water and gas and electricity, vehicles, vehicle fuel, protective insurance, housing, rent.

Examples:

B-6 Over-the-counter medicine has increased in price due to inflation. Each person feels the result of inflation because the cost of goods and services increases.

B-7 The price of a certain medicine has increased from \$2 to \$4. Calculate the percentage of price increase. $4 - 2 = 2$ divided by $2 = 1$, which is equal to the original 2, or 100% inflation

---

B-8 We could buy 90 toys for \$180.
Now the price for 90 toys is \$270.

Calculate the unit price per-toy: at \$180.

Calculate the unit price per-toy: at $270.
Calculate the percentage of price increase per toy as a result of inflation reducing our purchasing power.
Calculate the number of toys you can buy for $180 when priced at the new unit price. You will see that you have to purchase fewer toys with the limited amount of $180.

B-9 We could purchase 10 pieces of candy for $5.60.
Calculate the cost of each piece of candy.
Now the price for 8 pieces of candy is $5.60
Calculate the cost of each piece of candy at the new price.
This inflation-based price increase is hidden from most buyers.
It works because the quantity was reduced for the same number of pieces of candy.
The change is hidden because most buyers will be unaware.
Calculate the cost of each piece of candy at the new price structure.
Calculate the percentage price increase on one piece of candy.

.56   .70   .13   .23 or 23%

B-10 Vehicle oil change costs have been rising as costs of doing business rise for service centers. Rising cost may be insurance, labor, interest on business loan, supplies and more.

The last three service rate prices are:

$80
$100
$120

Calculate the dollar and percentage increase between each of the two as the cost rises

Calculate the dollar and percentage increase between the $80 and $120

Hint: the percentage increase is of the lower cost amount.

B-11 We came across a Flash Sale.
This is like the K-Mart Blue Light Special in the stores.

An $80 item is on sale today only for $60.

Calculate the dollar amount and the percentage of savings based on the original price to the discounted price.

$2/8 = 1/4 =$

B-12 We seek an excellent, knowledgeable and reliable service man.
We found such a service person.
His bill was $200.
We gave him $250 because we were pleased with his service.
We inflated our actual cost due to the quality of his service.

Calculate the extra number of dollars given as a tip.
Calculate the amount of the tip as a percentage of the bill.

B-13 The morning temperature is 50 degrees Fahrenheit and expected to reach 75 degrees during the day.

Calculate the rise in the temperature.
Calculate the percentage rise in the temperature over 50 degrees.
Calculate the percentage the morning temperature is of the high temperature for the day.

~~~~~~

You are invited to look across my author's bookshelf on the next pages. Perhaps, you may find a topic or an adventure story calling for your eyes to rest on and run across its pages to take you to a place possibly new or even distant for you.

AUTHOR'S BOOKSHELF

This book adds to the roster of resources available to you as the twelfth book sourcing my knowledge and experience for you.

My previous book is: Simple Math Workbook – Learning Essential Math Skills. It is directed to youth for they need the foundation of *simple math* to achieve and be successful – and so that they will not have to rely on artificial intelligence to solve problems for them.

Change Your Mindset and Enhance Your Future - Changing Behaviors and Habits Creates Your Future and Strengthens Family Life
https://www.amazon.com/dp/B09C42NQNJ
Published & LIVE August 7, 2021& #1 New Release
Your author writes this #1 New Release Self-help book offering discussion, which elevates to a higher level of thinking, as it moves from Section to Section focusing on age-related topics through college age to adulthood with the goal of supporting readers as they guide youth and themselves through their years of struggling, confusion and doubt. The book continues my passion to share my knowledge and experience offering guidance, discussion and choices about how the habits and patterns of life may be changed to create the way of life and better future desired by and for all family members.
The book is the fifth #1 New Release in my now-eleven-book Series: DREAMS FULFILLED.

Do you look for a Handbook and Workbook dedicated and speaking to Middle school Students published February 20, 2021 and
another to Teens in High School published January 26 2021 and another dedicated and speaking to College Students published February 14, 2021 to help them find their way?
The four books support you and your children and young adults in transition to new beginnings.
All four of these ranked # 1 New Release on Amazon.

Are you interested in a true story about a Boy Scouts Adventure?
Do you want to experience an Around-the-World Voyage from the comfort of your home?

Do you know a special person who would be excited to receive a book of Unique Recipes from days gone by?
Do you wonder what volunteers wrote about in their Inspirational Addresses in the past 75 years?

Are you in pursuit of a true story of Emigration to America testing the strength required to achieve The American Dream?

I write across genre in my Series *DREAMS FULFILLED*.
You may find the writing you seek on this, my Author Page.

Click the link below and make your choice:

https://www.amazon.com/Ralph-Koerber/e/B08MYQCQCS%3Fref=dbs_a_mng_rwt_scns_share

The central theme of my writings is the title of my Series: Dreams Fulfilled.
The dreams fulfilled are my life-long dreams of sharing my knowledge and experiences.
My writings address family values, adventures, motivational and self-help topics key to a more-broad and ever-encompassing way of living leading to joyfulness.

It is important for me to share my knowledge and experiences in the hope that the lives of readers will be enhanced, possibly enlightened, and possibly entertained when the adventures narrated take them to a place and experience far different from that they may know in their personal lives.
When this happens, my dreams are fulfilled.

So, each book is priced at Amazon minimum in the belief that readers will find value, buy and read.

My Series is different from other series, which are intended to offer and extend to the reader a continuing sequence of stories and play-outs of the characters through different parts of the same story in follow-on books. Each of my books is free-standing.

Please look at each book to see if it calls to you.

1. Road to Journey's End shares the story of a family journey of immigration and challenges to achieving The American Dream.
https://www.amazon.com/dp/B08MR33JYG LIVE November 5, 2020

2. Sail of a Lifetime shares a Caribbean Sailing Adventure with Boy Scouts.
https://www.amazon.com/dp/B08P9Y2BH3 LIVE December 5, 2020

Two books are about my volunteer Mother and her dedication to volunteering while being a Dedicated Mother and a fabulous cook.

3. Inspirational Invocations and Addresses, tells of her Selfless Volunteerism.
https://www.amazon.com/dp/B08PCNN3KZ LIVE December 5, 2020

4. Mother's Recipes - Family and Time-tested Specialties
https://www.amazon.com/dp/B08P9X4TBQ LIVE December 5, 2020
-----

5. Semester at Sea shares my amazing experiences on a floating college campus with 450 college students studying abroad for 110 days while circling the globe and visiting distant lands and cultures. The details of the unique voyage could be the drawing card for the reader or family member to become a study abroad student on Semester at Sea. That would be a life-changing and memorable semester.

https://www.amazon.com/dp/B08P913VCZ LIVE December 5, 2020

The next four Self-help books are important topical approaches for Middle School, High School Teens and College Students dealing with the pressures of today and for adults guiding their personal direction. Book Number nine speaks to the needs wants and desires of adults.

Each Self-help book has been Ranked # 1 New Release on Amazon.

6. Teen Handbook and Workbook - For Your New Life
https://www.amazon.com/dp/B08V4ZK2Q3 LIVE January 27, 2021 #1 New Release

7. College Student Handbook and Workbook - Guidance and Discussion
https://www.amazon.com/dp/B08WLJD8SK LIVE February 15, 2021# 1 New Release

8. Adult and Parent Handbook and Workbook - Guidance and Discussion
Supporting Middle School Families and Students
https://www.amazon.com/dp/B08X3VZBJ3 LIVE February 21, 2021 # 1 New Release

9. Adult Handbook and Workbook - A Discussion on Self-Improvement and Relationships
https://www.amazon.com/dp/B08Y4FJ7PM LIVE March 5, 2021 #1 New Release

10. Change Your Mindset and Enhance Your Future – Changing Behaviors and Habits Creates Your Future and Strengthens Family Life

https://www.amazon.com/dp/B09C42NQNJ LIVE August 6, 2021 #1 New Release

11. Simple Math Workbook – Learning Essential Math Skills

12. Now, this Simple Math Workbook for Adults November, 2022

Amazon Kindle and Paperback of each is available through Amazon.

More books are in process.

Your comments are welcome. rkwrite@yahoo.com

Please favor me with an Amazon Review.
The Review Link is on the lower left of the book's webpage.
Your Review is important and very much appreciated.
It helps share my story.
Reviews help bring my books to interested readers.

~~~~~~~~~~~~~~~~~~~~~~

Thank you for inviting me into your life and your mind.
It has been my privilege to share with you my knowledge
about *Simple Math* and I trust that you may continue to
expand your understanding of the perspectives and
principles of math to your personal benefit.

R. K.

Printed in Great Britain
by Amazon

43626863R00116